The Epicure's
Very Low
Carbohydrate
Cookbook

Marilyn Van Syckel

DAVID McKAY COMPANY, INC. · NEW YORK

The Epicure's Very Low Carbohydrate Cookbook

Affectionately dedicated to:
    Terry, Barbara, and Bloomingdale, for their encouragement, help, love, and especially their patience.

Acknowledgments to:
    Mark Limerick, for his guidance, humor, and editorial assistance;
    Sue Berkman, Home Economist, for her advice and editorial assistance;
    Edward P. H. Kern, for his editorial assistance;
    Composition of Foods, United States Department of Agriculture Handbook No. 8;
    Nutritive Value of Foods, United States Department of Agriculture, Home and Garden Bulletin #72, 1970.

Contents

Introduction

This book was created to come to the aid of the millions who have shed pounds on low carbohydrate diets such as the Atkins diet, the Stillman diet, and the Drinking Man's diet with spectacular success—but with nowhere to turn for exciting recipes for cooking low carbohydrate meals to *maintain* that cherished weight.

The monotony of the food required on other diets need not enter your conversation. "You can enjoy the widest variety of food on a very low carbohydrate diet," I've protested, "you don't have to miss a thing, not even bread or dessert." And I know! For years I have by choice (and not for weight reduction but because I personally believe it the healthiest and sensible way to eat) fed my family and friends low carbohydrate meals that are frankly wonderful and widely varied. If you were to eat lunch and dinner at my house, you would not take in more than 40 grams of carbohydrates. But you wouldn't be aware of it.

As a trained home economist, I've been able to alter the ingredients in some favorite and famous dishes and come up with recipes that while very low in carbohydrates are high in taste and sumptuous enough to serve at any meal or use when entertaining your fussiest guests. They taste gourmet, they sound gourmet—but all have been worked out to be prepared with a minimum of fuss and an awareness of the fact that a lot of cooks work, as I do, and carry many responsibilities besides doing duty in the kitchen.

Many of the recipes described here come from top restaurants in New York and San Francisco. I have selected their best and altered them with a strict eye to *minimal* carbohydrate content. Others I've developed myself. Once you learn the technique, by using this book, you can improvise endlessly yourself. Your only rule of thumb: include no more than 12 to 15 grams of carbohydrates in lunches, 25 in dinners. What you add to this gram count at breakfast is up to you and your doctor's recommendations as to what total you need daily. *Don't* try to eliminate too many carbohydrates to *maintain* your trim figure; our bodies need some every day.

In today's world most of us don't get enough exercise to use up all the carbohydrate that hard physical work once burned off. You'll find problem eaters in your family picking up their appetites at mealtime once you dispense with commercial snacks and the empty calories offered by the torrent of sweets and starches so many Americans grab at for a quick meal. The hardest of all human habits to change, most sociologists agree, are those surrounding food and sex, but both can be affected profoundly by the pleasure principle and that's a good part of what this book is about. It will show you how to prepare the best food you ever ate in the best way for your and your family's well-being in today's sedentary world.

Since I personally don't care for the taste or aftertaste of sugar substitutes, the recipes in the dessert chapter call for confectioners' or granulated sugar. Sugar, of course, is pure carbohydrate. Those of you on special diets or who don't mind using the substitutes can experiment with using these products in the quantities called for and thereby reduce the gram count even more. Don't forget that some sugar substitutes can't be added during cooking; simply stir in the desired amount after cooking, and enjoy.

You will find every kind of meal in this book and every category of food—appetizers for parties or dinners; hot and cold soups; entrées of all kinds; sauces for meats, seafood, desserts; egg dishes; vegetables; salads and salad dressings; breads, cookies, Yorkshire pudding, and (yes!) rich-tasting desserts.

Appetizers

One of the all-time threats to the American waistline is appetizers, particularly those served at cocktail parties or weddings on little rounds of bread and crackers, and before the main course at dinner.

Here are over thirty-five suggestions for ways to serve appetizers that are unusual and exciting but very low in carbohydrates. Fall, winter, spring, and summer cocktail party menus are provided in full; the recipes to accompany them follow. The second section describes delicious ways to prepare dinner appetizers and still keep the gram count within bounds.

PARTY APPETIZERS AND GARNISHES

COCKTAIL PARTY MENUS

Great imagination can be used when planning a large party, especially when you consider color and taste combinations.

FALL COCKTAIL PARTIES

Cubed Fontina cheese
Eggs stuffed with salmon*
Marinated mushrooms*
Italian meatballs*
Broiled shrimp and prosciutto*
Assorted raw vegetables with
   clam dip*

SPRING COCKTAIL PARTIES

Cubed feta cheese
Black olives
Eggs stuffed with mushrooms*
Greek meatballs*
Shrimp on artichoke leaves*
Assorted raw vegetables with
   curry-dill dip*

WINTER COCKTAIL PARTIES

Cubed Jarlsberg cheese
Smoked salmon rolls*
Raw mushrooms with caviar*
Swedish meatballs*
Rumaki*
Assorted raw vegetables with
   guacamole dip*

SUMMER COCKTAIL PARTIES

Cubed Tijuana cheese
Stuffed cucumbers*
Deviled eggs*
Steak tartare meatballs*
Lobster rumaki*
Assorted raw vegetables with
   California dip*

* Recipes are included for dishes starred.

COCKTAIL CHEESES

Here is a list of some semi-firm and firm cheeses that can be cubed and served easily with toothpicks. Each ¾ -inch cube is under .5 gram of carbohydrates.

Bonbel	Havarti
Bondost	Icelandic Banquet
Cheddar	Jarlsberg
Christian IX	La Grappe
Double Gloucester	Manchego
Edam	Muenster
Feta	Roquefort
Fontina	Samsø
Gorgonzola	Swiss
Gouda	Tijuana
Gruyère	Tilsiter

RAW VEGETABLES

Raw vegetables are delicious when dipped in party dips and each of these are under .5 gram of carbohydrates.

Very young asparagus spears	Peeled fennel (*finocchio*)
Broccoli flowerettes	Green pepper strips or rings
Peeled carrot sticks or curls	Whole green beans
Cauliflowerettes	Whole or sliced mushrooms
Celery sticks	Radish rosettes
Peeled celery root sticks	Scallions
Unpeeled cucumber sticks or slices	Cherry tomatoes
Small endive leaves	Peeled white turnip sticks
	Unpeeled zucchini sticks

CALIFORNIA DIP

MAKES 1½ CUPS .1 GRAM PER DIP

1 cup sour cream
1 package dried onion or leek
 soup mix

Salt, if needed

 Combine all ingredients and refrigerate 1 hour or longer.

CLAM DIP

MAKES 2 CUPS .1 GRAM PER DIP

1 3-ounce package cream
 cheese
¾ cup mayonnaise
1 8-ounce can minced clams,
 drained
⅛ teaspoon crushed garlic

¼ teaspoon salt
¼ teaspoon freshly ground
 pepper
¼ teaspoon paprika
1 teaspoon Worcestershire
 sauce

 Blend cream cheese and mayonnaise until smooth. Stir in remaining ingredients and refrigerate until chilled.

CURRY-DILL DIP

MAKES 1¼ CUPS 0 GRAMS PER DIP

1 cup mayonnaise
1 teaspoon fresh lemon or lime
 juice
¼ teaspoon onion juice
2 teaspoons curry powder

1 teaspoon dried or 2
 teaspoons fresh dill
¼ teaspoon seasoning salt
Freshly ground pepper

 Blend all ingredients until smooth. Chill 2 hours or longer.

GUACAMOLE DIP

MAKES 1½ CUPS   .1 GRAM PER DIP

2 large ripe avocados, pitted
1 tablespoon fresh lime or
   lemon juice
2 tablespoons chopped onions
⅛ teaspoon chopped garlic
6 tablespoons mayonnaise

½ teaspoon chili powder or hot
   red pepper flakes
¼ teaspoon salt
Freshly ground pepper
Cayenne pepper
2 drops Tabasco sauce

Combine all ingredients in electric blender. Cover and blend at high speed for 10 seconds. Scrape sides of blender with rubber spatula, and blend again until smooth. Pour into serving bowl and cover to prevent discoloration until ready to serve.

RAITA

MAKES 3½ CUPS   .1 GRAM PER DIP

1 large peeled cucumber
3 cups plain yogurt
1 tablespoon chopped onion
½ teaspoon salt
1 teaspoon cumin seeds

Freshly ground pepper
Cayenne pepper
1 tablespoon chopped fresh
   parsley

Combine cucumber, yogurt, onion, and salt in electric blender. Cover and blend at medium speed for 5 seconds. Scrape sides of blender with rubber spatula and blend again for 3 seconds. Toast cumin seeds in heavy skillet until they start to jump. Crush seeds with a mortar and pestle and stir half into chilled yogurt mixture. Refrigerate. Before serving, sprinkle with remaining toasted seeds, pepper, cayenne, and parsley.

STUFFED CUCUMBERS

MAKES 20 HORS D'OEUVRES .3 GRAM EACH

1 large unpeeled cucumber
1 3-ounce package cream cheese
1 tablespoon chopped chives
½ teaspoon chopped fresh parsley

1 teaspoon dry sherry
2 tablespoons mayonnaise
1 teaspoon paprika
Watercress

Cut cucumber in half crosswise and remove center with apple corer. Discard seeds. Combine remaining ingredients and mix until smooth. Fill hollow cucumber with cheese mixture and put two ends back together again. Refrigerate at least 2 hours or until thoroughly chilled.

Cut cucumber into ⅓-inch slices and arrange on bed of watercress on serving platter. Cover and chill until ready to serve.

DEVILED EGGS

MAKES 16 EGGS .2 GRAM EACH

8 hard-cooked eggs
3 tablespoons mayonnaise
¼ teaspoon dry mustard

¼ teaspoon curry powder (optional)
Salt and freshly ground pepper
3 sliced stuffed green olives

Split eggs lengthwise. Place yolks in a bowl and reserve whites. Combine mayonnaise, mustard, curry powder, salt, and pepper with yolks. Blend until very smooth. Spoon yolk mixture into egg whites and garnish with sliced olives. Cover and chill before serving.

EGGS STUFFED WITH MUSHROOMS
MAKES 16 EGGS .3 GRAM EACH

8 hard-cooked eggs
3 large chopped fresh
 mushrooms
1 tablespoon chopped scallions,
 including greens

1 tablespoon butter or
 margarine
1 tablespoon dry sherry
Salt and freshly ground pepper
Fresh parsley sprigs

Split eggs lengthwise. Place yolks in a bowl and reserve whites. Sauté mushrooms and scallions in butter until tender. Combine mushroom mixture with yolks and stir in sherry and salt and pepper. Blend until very smooth. Spoon yolk mixture into egg whites and garnish with parsley sprigs. Cover and chill before serving.

EGGS STUFFED WITH SALMON
MAKES 16 EGGS .4 GRAM EACH

8 hard-cooked eggs
¼ cup flaked salmon
½ teaspoon minced onion
3 tablespoons mayonnaise

1 tablespoon fresh lemon juice
Salt and cayenne pepper
1 thinly sliced pimiento

Split eggs lengthwise. Place yolks in a bowl and reserve whites. Combine salmon, onion, mayonnaise, lemon juice, salt, and pepper with yolks. Blend until very smooth. Spoon yolk mixture into egg whites and garnish with pimiento slices. Cover and chill before serving.

GREEK MEATBALLS

MAKES 45 MEATBALLS .2 GRAM EACH

1½ pounds ground lean round
    steak
¼ cup grated onions
¼ teaspoon crushed garlic
1 tablespoon chopped fresh
    or 1 teaspoon dried mint
¼ teaspoon crushed oregano
¼ teaspoon cinnamon

¼ teaspoon ground allspice
Salt and freshly ground pepper
1 tablespoon olive or
    vegetable oil
2 tablespoons fresh lemon
    juice
3 egg yolks, lightly beaten
1 cup chicken broth

Combine ground meat, onions, garlic, mint, oregano, cinnamon, allspice, salt, and pepper. Mix thoroughly with wet hands and shape into 1-inch meatballs. Brush bottom of cold skillet with oil, add meatballs in single layer and roll until evenly coated with oil. If Teflon skillet is used, no oil is necessary.

Place the skillet over high heat. Continue to roll meatballs with wooden spoon to prevent sticking. Reduce heat, if they start to stick, and sauté until evenly browned on all sides, about 5 minutes. Drain well. Continue cooking remaining meatballs without adding additional oil.

Combine lemon juice, egg yolks, and chicken broth in a chafing dish. Heat, without boiling, and stir until sauce thickens slightly. Reheat meatballs in sauce and serve with toothpicks.

ITALIAN MEATBALLS

MAKES 50 MEATBALLS .3 GRAM EACH

1½ pounds ground lean chuck
¼ cup finely grated onions
3 tablespoons freshly grated
    Parmesan cheese
½ teaspoon minced garlic
1 tablespoon chopped fresh
    parsley

Cayenne pepper
Salt and freshly ground pepper
1 tablespoon olive or
    vegetable oil
1 8-ounce jar Marinara sauce

Combine ground meat, onions, cheese, garlic, parsley, cay-enne pepper, salt, and pepper. Mix thoroughly with wet hands and shape into 1-inch meatballs. Brush bottom of cold skillet with oil, add meatballs in single layer and roll until evenly coated with oil. If Teflon skillet is used, no oil is necessary. Place skillet over high heat. Continue to roll meatballs with wooden spoon to prevent sticking. Reduce heat, if they start to stick, and sauté them until evenly browned on all sides, about 5 minutes. Drain well. Continue cooking remaining meatballs without adding additional oil.

Reheat meatballs in a chafing dish in Marinara sauce and serve with toothpicks.

STEAK TARTARE MEATBALLS
MAKES 60 MEATBALLS   0 GRAMS EACH

2 pounds freshly ground lean round steak	2 dashes Tabasco sauce
1 teaspoon fresh lime juice	½ teaspoon dry mustard
2 tablespoons dry red wine	Salt and freshly ground pepper
⅛ teaspoon crushed garlic	Capers or small Dutch cocktail onions

Have butcher trim *all* fat from round steak and grind twice. Combine ground steak, lime juice, wine, garlic, Tabasco, mus-tard, salt, and pepper. Mix thoroughly with wet hands and shape into 1-inch meatballs. Spear one or two capers or onions and then meatball with toothpick. Refrigerate at least 1 hour, but not longer than 3 hours, before serving.

SWEDISH MEATBALLS

MAKES 45 MEATBALLS .3 GRAM EACH

1 pound ground lean round
    steak
¼ pound ground lean pork
¼ pound ground veal
1 egg, lightly beaten
2 tablespoons grated onions
½ teaspoon grated lemon rind
½ teaspoon fresh lemon juice
½ teaspoon chopped fresh or
    ⅛ teaspoon dried dill

½ teaspoon salt
Freshly ground pepper
1 tablespoon olive or
    vegetable oil
1 can consommé, undiluted
1 tablespoon flour
2 tablespoons butter or
    margarine
1 tablespoon dry sherry
1 cup sour cream

Combine ground meats, egg, onions, lemon rind, lemon juice, dill, salt, and pepper. Mix thoroughly with wet hands and shape into 1-inch meatballs. Brush bottom of cold skillet with oil, add meatballs in single layer and roll until evenly coated with oil. If Teflon skillet is used, no oil is necessary. Place skillet over high heat. Continue to roll meatballs with wooden spoon to prevent sticking. Reduce heat, if they start to stick, and sauté until evenly browned on all sides, about 5 minutes. Drain well. Continue cooking remaining meatballs without adding additional oil.

Bring consommé to a rapid boil. Drop drained meatballs into consommé, reduce heat, simmer 15 minutes. Remove meatballs to a chafing dish. Wipe the skillet with paper towel. Brown flour in butter and stir in consommé. Simmer over low heat and stir until sauce thickens slightly. At serving time, stir in sherry and sour cream and heat, without boiling. Reheat meatballs in sauce in chafing dish and serve with toothpicks.

RAW MUSHROOMS WITH CAVIAR

MAKES 50 MUSHROOMS .5 GRAM EACH

1 pound small raw mushrooms
1 cup sour cream

1 4-ounce jar black caviar

Carefully wipe and trim mushrooms. Remove and mince stems. Combine minced stems with sour cream and spoon equal portion of mixture into each cap. Mound caviar on top of sour cream and chill until ready to serve.

MARINATED MUSHROOMS
MAKES 50 MUSHROOMS   .3 GRAM EACH

1 pound small fresh mushrooms
½ cup wine vinegar
2 tablespoons olive or vegetable oil
½ teaspoon crushed oregano
1 tablespoon chopped fresh parsley
1 garlic clove, halved
½ teaspoon salt
Freshly ground pepper

Thoroughly wash and trim mushrooms, leaving stems intact. Boil mushrooms in salted water to cover for 5 minutes. Drain. Combine remaining ingredients with mushrooms in a large jar, cover, and refrigerate 3 hours or overnight. Discard the garlic. Serve mushrooms on toothpicks surrounded with fresh parsley or watercress.

MUSHROOMS STUFFED WITH ANCHOVIES
MAKES 16 MUSHROOMS   1.6 GRAMS EACH

16 large mushrooms
2 tablespoons olive or vegetable oil
¼ teaspoon minced garlic
1 2½-ounce can anchovy fillets
¼ cup minced cooked chicken
1 teaspoon lemon juice
2 tablespoons chopped fresh parsley
Freshly ground pepper
2 tablespoons fine bread crumbs
1 tablespoon butter or margarine

Carefully wipe and trim mushrooms. Remove and chop stems. Pour oil in a heavy skillet and roll mushroom caps until evenly coated. Place them in a greased baking dish and set aside. Sauté chopped stems and garlic for 1 minute in same skillet. Drain, rinse, and chop anchovies and stir into skillet with chicken, lemon juice, parsley, and pepper. Spoon anchovy mixture into each mushroom cap, sprinkle with bread crumbs, and dot with butter. Preheat oven to 350° F. and bake mushrooms 15 minutes or until lightly browned. Serve individually as hors d'oeuvres or as a garnish for fish.

STUFFED MUSHROOMS PARMIGIANA
MAKES 16 MUSHROOMS   1.4 GRAMS EACH

16 large fresh mushrooms
2 tablespoons olive or
   vegetable oil
2 tablespoons minced onions
½ teaspoon minced garlic
2 tablespoons Madeira or dry
   sherry
½ cup freshly grated imported
   Parmesan cheese

¼ cup minced cooked chicken,
   ham, or shrimp
2 tablespoons chopped fresh
   parsley
¼ teaspoon tarragon
2 tablespoons heavy cream
Salt and freshly ground pepper
2 tablespoons butter or
   margarine

Carefully wipe and trim mushrooms. Remove and chop stems. Pour oil in a heavy skillet and roll mushroom caps until evenly coated. Place them in a greased baking dish and set aside. Sauté chopped stems, onions, and garlic in same skillet, until onions are tender. Set mixture aside. Add wine to skillet, boil until almost dry, scraping sides and bottom of pan. Turn off heat. Add onion mixture and stir in cheese, meat, parsley, tarragon, cream, salt, and pepper. Spoon cheese mixture into each mushroom cap and dot with butter.

Preheat oven to 350° F. and bake mushrooms 15 minutes or until lightly browned. Serve individually as hors d'oeuvres or as a garnish for meat.

RUMAKI

MAKES 45 HORS D'OEUVRES .8 GRAM EACH

1 cup soy sauce
½ cup chicken broth
1 bay leaf
1 cinnamon stick

⅛ teaspoon crushed garlic
1 pound fresh chicken livers
1 can water chestnuts, sliced
½ pound bacon, cut in thirds

Combine soy sauce, chicken broth, bay leaf, cinnamon, and garlic. Bring to a boil, reduce heat and simmer 5 minutes. Discard cinnamon stick. Add chicken livers and simmer 10 minutes. Drain, cool, and cut livers in thirds. Wrap bacon around a piece of liver and water chestnut and secure with toothpick.

Preheat broiler and slowly broil rumaki on slotted broiler pan about 4 inches from heat for 5 minutes or until golden brown on all sides. Keep warm until ready to serve.

LOBSTER RUMAKI

MAKES 45 HORS D'OEUVRES .5 GRAM EACH

1 pound raw firm lobster meat
¼ cup soy sauce
¼ cup dry sherry

1 can water chestnuts, sliced
½ pound bacon, cut in thirds

Cut lobster meat in ½-inch-thick pieces about the diameter of water chestnuts. Combine soy sauce, sherry, and lobster and marinate in refrigerator 1 hour or longer. Drain. Wrap bacon around a piece of lobster and water chestnut and secure with toothpick.

Preheat oven to 400° F. and bake rumaki on slotted broiler pan 10 minutes or until bacon is golden brown on all sides. Keep warm until ready to serve.

SMOKED SALMON ROLLS

MAKES 50 HORS D'OEUVRES .1 GRAM EACH

10 thin slices smoked salmon
Fresh lemon juice
1 3-ounce package cream
 cheese
2 tablespoons sour cream

¼ teaspoon dried or ½
 teaspoon fresh dill
Coarsely ground pepper
1 tablespoon chopped capers,
 drained

Sprinkle slices of salmon with lemon juice. Combine cream cheese, sour cream, and dill. Spread thin layer over entire surface of salmon. Sprinkle with pepper and capers. Roll salmon, cover, and refrigerate, seam side down, for 2 hours of longer. Slice salmon rolls into ¾-inch pieces and serve on toothpicks.

SHRIMP ON ARTICHOKE LEAVES

MAKES 50 HORS D'OEUVRES .2 GRAM EACH

1 large cooked artichoke
1 cup mayonnaise
1 tablespoon curry powder

Seasoned salt
1 pound tiny bay shrimp
1 large uncooked artichoke

Separate leaves from cooked artichoke. Combine mayonnaise, curry powder, and salt. Place ¼ teaspoon of mixture on edible part of artichoke leaf and top with one or more shrimp. Arrange assembled leaves on a platter surrounding neatly trimmed raw artichoke that has been brushed with lemon juice to prevent discoloration. Serve chilled.

BROILED SHRIMP AND PROSCIUTTO
MAKES 50 HORS D'OEUVRES .2 GRAM EACH

2 pounds large raw shrimp
½ cup cognac or brandy
½ teaspoon marjoram or sweet
  basil
½ teaspoon salt

¼ teaspoon freshly ground
  pepper
½ pound thinly sliced
  prosciutto, ham, or bacon

Carefully clean raw shrimp by removing shells and vein. Combine cognac, marjoram, salt, and pepper and pour over cleaned shrimp. Cover and marinate in refrigerator for 1 hour or longer. Drain shrimp and wrap in a 1-by-3-inch strip of prosciutto and secure with toothpick.

Preheat broiler and broil shrimp on a slotted broiler pan about 4 inches from heat for 5 minutes or until golden brown on all sides. Serve hot or cold.

DINNER APPETIZERS

ANTIPASTO
MAKES 8 SERVINGS   3.8 GRAMS PER SERVING

2 small cans Italian tuna fish
8 thin slices prosciutto
8 thin slices Italian salami
8 anchovy fillets
4 small celery hearts, cut in
  half lengthwise
16 large green olives

16 black ripe olives
8 small marinated artichoke
  hearts
4 pimiento pods, halved
8 slices peeled tomatoes
8 Tuscan vinegar peppers

   Center tuna fish chunk on large individual salad plates and arrange remaining ingredients attractively around.

CRAB COCKTAIL
MAKES 8 SERVINGS   1.3 GRAMS PER SERVING

1 cup mayonnaise
1/2 teaspoon minced garlic
1 1/2 teaspoons fresh lime juice
2 tablespoons prepared hot
  mustard
1 tablespoon A-1 steak sauce

3/4 teaspoon crushed dried
  tarragon
1/8 teaspoon Angostura bitters
1 1/2 teaspoons brandy (optional)
1 1/2 pounds cooked crab or
  lobster meat

17

Combine all ingredients (except crab meat) and refrigerate for 1 hour or longer. Before serving, gently toss sauce with crab meat and serve on a bed of lettuce or in compotes with shredded lettuce.

EGGS IN ASPIC

MAKES 8 SERVINGS   1.0 GRAM PER SERVING

8 large eggs	Salt and freshly ground pepper
2 cups beef bouillon	2 envelopes unflavored gelatin
½ cup V-8 juice	Tarragon leaves or trimmed
2 eggshells	scallion greens
2 tablespoons cognac	8 round slices boiled ham
1 sprig of fresh or 1 teaspoon	Watercress
dried tarragon	

Poach eggs in a poacher (so they will be round) until their centers are soft and the whites firm. Combine bouillon, V-8 juice, eggshells, cognac, tarragon, salt, and pepper, and boil for 5 minutes. Strain. Dissolve gelatin in aspic and pour into eight individual molds or custard cups. Chill 10 minutes and pour unset aspic off and reserve. Place two green tarragon leaves or trimmed scallion greens in a V-shape on partially set aspic. Add poached eggs and top with ham rounds. Pour in remaining chilled but still-liquid aspic and chill until firm.

Before serving, unmold by quickly dipping outside of mold in hot water. Place on a bed of lettuce and garnish with watercress.

EGGS À LA RUSSE

MAKES 8 SERVINGS   .7 GRAM PER SERVING

8 hard-cooked eggs	1 tablespoon light cream
1 cup Hollandaise sauce (see	Sliced truffles
Sauces)	

Carefully peel hard-cooked eggs and cut in half lengthwise. Arrange two halves, cut side down, on individual serving plates. Combine Hollandaise sauce with cream and pour over eggs. Serve garnished with sliced truffles.

ESCARGOTS

MAKES 8 SERVINGS   1.4 GRAMS PER SERVING

¼ pound softened sweet
   butter
1½ teaspoons minced garlic
2 tablespoons minced fresh
   parsley

Pinch freshly grated nutmeg
Freshly ground white pepper
4 dozen snail shells
4 dozen imported canned
   snails

Cream butter, garlic, parsley, nutmeg, and pepper together until smooth. Set aside for 1 hour (for a stronger garlic flavor, set aside at least 2 hours or refrigerate overnight).

Preheat oven to 350° F. Spoon some softened butter mixture into each shell; follow by adding one snail and fill with more butter. Arrange shells on individual escargot plates and bake 12 minutes. Serve sizzling hot escargots on their plates on top of a dinner platter.

CHOPPED CHICKEN LIVERS

MAKES 8 SERVINGS   3.1 GRAMS PER SERVING

1 pound chicken livers
1 medium onion, quartered
1 cup chicken broth
½ cup minced onions
1 tablespoon vegetable oil
4 chopped hard-cooked eggs
2 tablespoons rendered
   chicken fat

1 teaspoon salt
¼ teaspoon freshly ground
   pepper
Cherry tomatoes
Large imported cocktail onions
Watercress

Drop chicken livers and quartered onion into boiling chicken broth. Cook 5 minutes or until livers are just tender. Drain, discarding onion and broth, and cool livers. Sauté minced onion in oil until tender. Mash livers and eggs until smooth. Blend in chicken fat to consistency of mashed potatoes. Stir in sautéed onions and the salt and pepper. Serve at room temperature garnished with tomatoes, cocktail onions, and watercress.

MOULES RAVIGOTE
MAKES 8 SERVINGS   6.2 GRAMS PER SERVING

4 quarts fresh mussels	½ bay leaf
1½ cups dry white wine	½ teaspoon thyme
1 cup water	Cayenne pepper
2 shallots, quartered	Salt and freshly ground pepper
2 small onions, quartered	2 cups *sauce ravigote* (see
2 tablespoons butter or	*Sauces*)
margarine	Freshly ground white pepper
2 fresh parsley sprigs	

Scrub mussels with stiff brush to remove all sand and beards. Refrigerate until ready to use. Boil wine, water, shallot and onion quarters, butter, parsley sprigs, bay leaf, thyme, cayenne, salt, and pepper in a large kettle for 5 minutes. Add mussels, cover, and bring to a rapid boil again. Boil 5 to 10 minutes. Lift and stir mussels occasionally. Remove mussels from broth. Discard all unopened shells. Remove meat from shells and set aside.

Strain 1 cup of broth through cloth-lined sieve and bring to a rapid boil and reduce to ½ cup. Cool to room temperature. Make 2 cups of *sauce ravigote* (see *Sauces*), using ½ cup of reduced broth instead of wine. Pour sauce over shelled mussels and sprinkle with freshly ground pepper. Serve at room temperature on lettuce.

MUSHROOMS À LA GRECQUE

MAKES 8 SERVINGS   5.6 GRAMS PER SERVING

2 cups water
½ cup olive or vegetable oil
¼ cup fresh lemon juice
1 tablespoon minced shallots
1 garlic clove, halved
6 sprigs fresh parsley
1 sliced celery stalk with leaves
1 sprig fresh fennel or ⅛ teaspoon fennel seed
½ teaspoon dried thyme
10 peppercorns
6 coriander seeds or ¾ teaspoon ground coriander
1 teaspoon salt
2 pounds fresh small mushrooms
Chopped fresh parsley or coriander leaves

Combine all ingredients (except mushrooms and chopped parsley) in a large enamel or stainless steel saucepan. Bring to a boil, cover and simmer 10 minutes. Add mushrooms, cover and simmer 8 minutes longer. Remove mushrooms and set aside. Bring liquid to a rapid boil and reduce to ⅓ cup. Strain liquid over mushrooms, cover, and refrigerate overnight. Serve mushrooms individually as hors d'oeuvres or on shredded lettuce in compotes as an appetizer garnished with parsley.

OYSTERS CASINO

MAKES 8 SERVINGS   3.5 GRAMS PER SERVING

4 slices bacon
⅔ cup minced scallions, including greens
⅓ cup minced green pepper
⅓ cup minced celery
1¼ teaspoons fresh lemon juice
1¼ teaspoons Worcestershire sauce
3 drops Tabasco
4 dozen medium oysters on the half shell
Rock salt

Cook bacon until crisp and drain well. Sauté scallions, green peppers, and celery in 2 tablespoons of bacon drippings until tender. Season with lemon juice, Worcestershire, and Tabasco. Place two drained oysters on one shell. Spoon sautéed mixture over oysters and sprinkle with crumbled bacon. Place shells on a bed of rock salt in a shallow baking pan.

Preheat oven to 400° F. and bake 10 minutes or until sauce bubbles. Serve piping hot.

OYSTERS ROCKEFELLER
MAKES 8 SERVINGS   3.4 GRAMS PER SERVING

1 cup (firmly packed) young spinach leaves	2 tablespoons Pernod
¼ cup chopped scallions, including greens	Dash Tabasco
¼ cup chopped fresh parsley	Salt and freshly ground pepper
¼ cup chopped celery	¼ pound melted sweet butter or margarine
¼ teaspoon chopped garlic	4 dozen medium oysters on the half shell
¼ teaspoon tarragon	Rock salt
¼ teaspoon chervil	

Blend spinach, scallions, parsley, celery, garlic, tarragon, chervil, Pernod, Tabasco, salt, and pepper in electric blender on high speed until smooth. Occasionally scrape sides of blender with rubber spatula. Cover blender and turn motor on again. Remove cover and slowly pour in melted butter. Turn motor off immediately.

Spoon sauce over each oyster on the half shell and spread sauce to rim of shell.

Preheat oven to 450° F. Place shells on a bed of rock salt in shallow baking pan. Bake 10 minutes or until sauce bubbles. Serve piping hot.

PROSCIUTTO AND MELON
MAKES 8 SERVINGS   4.2 GRAMS PER SERVING

2 ripe melons (cantaloupe, Casaba, honeydew, or Persian)
½ pound thinly sliced prosciutto ham

Fresh lemon juice
Coarsely ground pepper or lemon-pepper marinade
8 lemon wedges

Cut melons in quarters. Discard seeds and rind. Slice each wedge lengthwise into ½-inch thick wedges and lay them side by side on individual serving plates. Sprinkle with lemon juice. Remove fat from prosciutto and arrange meat over sliced melon. Chill until ready to serve. Serve garnished with lemon wedges and accompanied by pepper mill (set for coarse grinding) or with a shaker of lemon-pepper marinade.

NOTE: This can also be served as an hors d'oeuvre (.3 gram each). Cube melon, sprinkle with lemon juice, and wrap in 1-by-3-inch slices of prosciutto and spear with toothpicks.

SEAFOOD IN SHELLS
MAKES 8 SERVINGS   2.5 GRAMS PER SERVING

8 clams on the half shell
32 empty large clam shells
2 cups seafood sauce (see Sauces)
1 cup cooked crab meat chunks
1 cup cooked shrimp chunks

1 cup cooked lobster chunks
½ pound smoked salmon, cut in bite-size pieces
8 lemon wedges
Watercress or fresh parsley

Fill eight large flat soup plates with crushed ice. Equally space a clam on its shell and 4 empty clam shells in circle around small container of seafood sauce. Fill empty shells individually: 1 with crab, 1 with shrimp, 1 with lobster, and 1 with salmon. Serve each plate with lemon wedge and garnish with watercress or fresh parsley.

Soups

Why make it when you can buy it? Because it's better! And because all commercial soups contain carbohydrates and other ingredients you probably never realized were in those innocent-looking cans or packages. Many are thickened with starches, flavored with sugars, and their contents made stable and lasting with some surprising ingredients and chemicals.

The fifteen soups that follow are all made of natural ingredients, are low in carbohydrates, and taste sensational. Some are so filling that you could very well make them the mainstay of a soup-and-salad dinner. There are hot soups for cold nights and cold soups for warm nights, or to start a filling meal.

HOT SOUPS

AVGOLEMONO SOUP

MAKES 8 SERVINGS 3.4 GRAMS PER SERVING

6 cups chicken broth
2½ tablespoons raw rice
5 tablespoons fresh lemon
   juice
4 large eggs, well beaten

Salt and freshly ground white
   pepper
2 tablespoons minced fresh
   mint

Bring chicken broth to a rapid boil in large enamel or stainless steel saucepan. Add rice and stir. Cover, lower heat, and simmer 20 minutes or until rice is very soft. Remove pan from heat. Gradually beat lemon juice and 4 tablespoons of warm broth into eggs. Slowly pour mixture into soup. Simmer, but do not boil, for 3 minutes or until slightly thickened. Add salt, white pepper, and more lemon juice, if needed. To serve, reheat, without boiling, and sprinkle with chopped mint.

CONSOMMÉ WITH QUENELLES

MAKES 8 SERVINGS 1.6 GRAMS PER SERVING

⅓ pound finely ground veal
2 egg whites, lightly beaten
¼ cup heavy cream
¾ teaspoon curry powder
½ teaspoon salt

Freshly ground white pepper
6 cups bouillon
1 tablespoon quick-cooking
   tapioca
2 leeks, cut in julienne strips

Thoroughly mix veal with egg whites. Add cream, curry, salt, and pepper and mix again. With wet hands shape meat into 1-inch meatballs (quenelles). Bring bouillon to a rolling boil and slowly add quenelles. Sprinkle with tapioca and sliced leeks, lower heat, and simmer 10 minutes. Serve piping hot.

EGG-DROP SOUP

MAKES 8 SERVINGS .3 GRAM PER SERVING

½ pound very lean pork, cut in
   julienne strips
1 tablespoon soy sauce
1 teaspoon dry sherry

6 cups chicken broth or beef
   bouillon
½ teaspoon salt
2 eggs, lightly beaten

Combine pork strips with soy sauce and sherry. Marinate 10 to 15 minutes. Bring broth to a rapid boil and stir in salt. Gradually add pork strips so as not to stop boiling. Boil 2 minutes. Very slowly pour eggs into boiling soup, stirring constantly. Immediately remove saucepan from heat so eggs will shred into "petals." Serve piping hot.

ONION SOUP

MAKES 8 SERVINGS 6.4 GRAMS PER SERVING

3 cups thinly sliced onions
2 tablespoons olive or
   vegetable oil
2 tablespoons butter or
   margarine
8 cups strong beef bouillon

1 cup dry red wine
1 bay leaf
Salt and freshly ground pepper
1½ cups freshly grated
   Parmesan cheese

Slice onions on the bias to avoid rings and sauté them in oil and butter in large kettle until tender and browned. Add bouillon, wine, bay leaf, salt, and pepper. Stir, scraping sides and bottom of kettle, and simmer 30 minutes. Discard bay leaf and refrigerate overnight. Reheat and serve piping hot. Garnish with Parmesan cheese served separately.

PETITE MARMITE
MAKES 8 SERVINGS 2.5 GRAMS PER SERVING

2 pounds meaty soup bones
4 cups chicken broth
4 cans beef bouillon, undiluted
1 pound lean chuck fillet
1 celery stalk
1 small onion stuck with
 1 clove
¼ teaspoon minced garlic
½ bay leaf
⅛ teaspoon thyme
4 peppercorns or ¼ teaspoon
 cracked pepper

½ cup peeled sliced carrots
¼ cup peeled cubed white
 turnips
¼ cup sliced leeks, white part
 only
1 cup cubed cooked white
 chicken meat (optional)
Salt, if needed
Freshly grated Gruyère cheese
 or lemon rind
8 large raw mushroom slices
 (optional)

Cover soup bones with water, bring to a boil, and simmer 10 minutes. Discard water and rinse bones thoroughly under cold running water. Combine broth, bouillon, two cans of water, chuck fillet, celery, onion, garlic, and spices in heavy kettle with the soup bones. Bring to a boil, cover, and simmer over very low heat for 1 hour or until meat is tender when tested with a fork. Strain broth, reserving chuck fillet. Cut the fillet into ½-inch cubes and set aside.

To strained broth, add carrots, turnips, and leeks. Bring to a boil, cover and simmer 20 minutes or until vegetables are tender. Skim off fat. Add cubes of meat and heat thoroughly. Serve in earthenware ramekins. Garnish with grated cheese (served separately), lemon rind, or sliced mushrooms.

PHILADELPHIA SNAPPER SOUP

MAKES 8 SERVINGS   4.1 GRAMS PER SERVING

1½ tablespoons flour
2 tablespoons corn oil
3 cups beef bouillon
6 tablespoons tomato purée
5 cups water
1 cup clam juice
1 cup dry white wine
1 onion stuck with 2 cloves
6 peppercorns
½ bay leaf
2 sprigs parsley

½ cup sliced, peeled carrots
⅛ teaspoon thyme
1½ teaspoons salt
¼ cup minced onions
½ cup minced celery
½ cup minced green peppers
2 tablespoons butter or margarine
1 cup diced red snapper
½ cup dry sherry

Brown flour in oil and add bouillon and tomato purée. Stir and boil 30 minutes or until liquid is reduced to 2 cups. Combine water, clam juice, wine, cloved onion, peppercorns, bay leaf, parsley, carrots, thyme and salt in a large kettle. Simmer 30 minutes. Strain and bring to a rapid boil, reduce to 4 cups. Combine with tomato bouillon. Sauté minced onions, celery, and green peppers in butter until tender. Stir into soup and bring to a rapid boil. Add red snapper and boil gently 12 minutes or until fish is just tender when tested with a fork. At serving time, reheat soup, add sherry, and serve piping hot.

COLD SOUPS

CAVIAR MADRILÈNE

MAKES 8 SERVINGS   3.3 GRAMS PER SERVING

4 cans jellied Madrilène
8 teaspoons caviar
¾ cup sour cream

3 teaspoons chopped chives
Fresh lemon or lime wedges
(optional)

Spoon jellied Madrilène into eight individual chilled soup bowls. Stir 1 teaspoon of caviar into each bowl and top with heaping tablespoon of sour cream. Sprinkled with chopped chives and garnish with lemon or lime wedges, if desired.

COLD CURRIED AVOCADO SOUP

MAKES 8 SERVINGS   3.5 GRAMS PER SERVING

2 cups cubed avocado meat
4 cups chicken broth
2 teaspoons curry powder
2 drops Tabasco sauce
1 teaspoon salt

⅛ teaspoon freshly ground
    white pepper
1 cup heavy cream
8 thin lemon slices
1 tablespoon chopped chives
    or fresh dill

Blend avocado, 1 cup of broth, curry, Tabasco, salt, and pepper in electric blender at high speed for 15 seconds. Occa-

31

sionally scrape sides of blender with rubber spatula. Combine avocado mixture with remaining broth in enamel saucepan, heat, and stir until soup comes to a boil. Cool slightly. Stir in cream and chill. Serve chilled in soup bowls garnished with thin lemon slices sprinkled with chopped chives or dill.

GAZPACHO

MAKES 8 SERVINGS   7.8 GRAMS PER SERVING

½ teaspoon chopped garlic	2 tablespoons wine vinegar
½ cup sliced onions	2 tablespoons olive oil
½ cup sliced peeled cucumber	⅛ teaspoon salt
1½ cups peeled, seeded tomatoes	⅛ teaspoon cayenne pepper
	½ cup diced onions
½ cup sliced green peppers	½ cup diced cucumbers
½ cup sliced celery	½ cup diced peeled, seeded tomatoes
4 eggs	
1 cup V-8 juice	½ cup diced green peppers

Purée all ingredients (except diced vegetables) in electric blender at high speed. Occasionally scrape sides of blender with rubber spatula. Cover and chill 1 hour or longer. At serving time, garnish soup with diced vegetables in individual soup bowls surrounded with crushed ice.

SENEGALESE SOUP

MAKES 8 SERVINGS   6.6 GRAMS PER SERVING

1 cup chopped onions	4 cups chicken broth
½ cup chopped celery	1 bay leaf
1 tablespoon butter or margarine	1 egg yolk, lightly beaten
	1 cup light cream, chilled
1 tablespoon flour	Cayenne pepper
1 tablespoon curry powder	Salt and freshly ground white pepper
1 cup diced, peeled tart apples	
1 cup diced cooked chicken	Coriander leaves

Sauté onions and celery in butter until tender. Stir in flour and curry and simmer 2 minutes. Blend onion mixture, apples, chicken, and 1 cup of chicken broth in electric blender at high speed for 15 seconds or until smooth. Occasionally scrape sides of blender with rubber spatula.

Combine chicken purée, remaining broth, and bay leaf and bring soup to a boil. Discard bay leaf and chill.

At serving time, combine egg yolk with cream and add to chilled soup. Season with cayenne, salt, and pepper and garnish with coriander leaves.

COLD TOMATO SOUP
MAKES 8 SERVINGS 7.3 GRAMS PER SERVING

3 cups tomato juice
2 tablespoons tomato paste
1 cup sour cream
1 cup chicken broth
2 tablespoons chopped shallots
¼ teaspoon thyme
½ teaspoon curry powder
1 tablespoon chopped lemon rind

2 tablespoons fresh lemon juice
1 tablespoon Worcestershire sauce
1 teaspoon sugar or sugar substitute
Salt and freshly ground pepper
Thin lemon slices
Chopped fresh parsley or chives

Blend 1 cup of tomato juice with remaining ingredients (except lemon slices and chopped parsley) in electric blender at medium speed for 30 seconds or until smooth. Occasionally scrape sides of blender with rubber spatula. Stir in remaining tomato juice and refrigerate overnight.

At serving time, garnish each portion with slice of lemon sprinkled with parsley or chives.

HOT OR COLD SOUPS

BILLI BI

MAKES 8 SERVINGS   5.0 GRAMS PER SERVING

2 quarts fresh mussels
1½ cups dry white wine
2 cups clam juice or
   fish stock
2 cups water
½ cup chopped onions
2 tablespoons chopped
   shallots
2 tablespoons chopped fresh
   parsley
½ bay leaf

½ teaspoon thyme
2 tablespoons melted butter
   or margarine
1 cup heavy cream
5 egg yolks, lightly beaten
1 tablespoon fresh lemon
   juice
Dash cayenne pepper
Freshly ground pepper
Salt (if needed)
3 tablespoons chopped chives

Scrub mussels with stiff brush to remove all sand and beards. Refrigerate until ready to use.

Boil wine, clam juice, water, onions, shallots, parsley, bay leaf, and thyme in large kettle for 5 minutes. Add mussels, cover, and bring to rapid boil again. Boil 5 to 10 minutes. Lift and stir mussels occasionally. Remove mussels from broth. Discard all unopened shells. Remove meat from shells and reserve as garnish.

Strain the broth through cloth-lined sieve, bring to a rapid boil and reduce to 4 cups. Combine butter, cream, and egg yolks. Slowly add to hot broth. Stir and heat, without boiling, until soup thickens slightly. Add lemon juice, cayenne, pepper, salt (if needed), and mussels. Continue heating, without boiling, for 2 minutes. Serve hot or cold, sprinkled with chopped chives.

BORSCHT
MAKES 8 SERVINGS 5.4 GRAMS PER SERVING

5 cups strong beef bouillon
1 large cabbage leaf
1 pound can julienne beets
  with juice
1 teaspoon vinegar

1 teaspoon sugar or sugar
  substitute (if needed)
Salt and freshly ground pepper
½ cup sour cream
1 tablespoon chopped fresh
  dill or parsley

Bring bouillon to a boil, add cabbage leaf, lower heat, and simmer 20 minutes. Discard cabbage leaf. Add beet juice, half of beets, vinegar, and sugar (if needed). Simmer over medium heat 15 minutes. Add remaining beets, salt, and pepper.

To serve hot, stir 2 tablespoons of soup broth into sour cream. Add mixture a little at a time to soup and heat, without boiling. Garnish with dill or parsley.

To serve cold, chill soup and add sour cream just before serving. Garnish with dill or parsley.

LOBSTER BISQUE
MAKES 8 SERVINGS 6.2 GRAMS PER SERVING

½ cup chopped onions
1 tablespoon butter or
  margarine
3 tablespoons flour
1½ cups milk
1 cup chicken broth
½ cup dry white wine
½ teaspoon paprika

1 teaspoon salt
Cayenne pepper
¼ cup warmed brandy
1 pound cubed cooked lobster
  meat
Red food coloring (optional)
1 cup heavy cream
Minced chives

Sauté onions in butter until tender. Sprinkle with flour and gradually stir in milk, chicken broth, wine, paprika, salt, and cayenne. Stir and cook until thickened.

Pour brandy over lobster meat in saucepan, ignite, and, when flame dies, heat slowly 5 minutes.

Add thickened sauce and simmer 5 minutes. Reserve some large pieces of lobster meat. Pour soup into electric blender and blend at high speed for 20 seconds or until soup is smooth. Occasionally scrape sides of blender with rubber spatula. Add food coloring, if desired. Chill at least 3 hours.

At serving time, add cream and beat 1 minute. Add reserved lobster meat and heat, without boiling, or serve chilled. Garnish with minced chives.

CREAM OF WATERCRESS SOUP
MAKES 8 SERVINGS 3.8 GRAMS PER SERVING

⅓ cup chopped scallions, including greens
2 tablespoons butter or margarine
4 packed cups chopped watercress
½ teaspoon salt

Freshly ground pepper
2 tablespoons flour
5 cups chicken broth
3 egg yolks
½ cup heavy cream
Green food coloring (optional)
Watercress leaves

Sauté scallions in butter until tender. Stir in watercress and sprinkle with salt and pepper. Cover and simmer 5 minutes. Sprinkle with flour and stir in 1 cup of chicken broth and simmer 3 minutes. Pour into electric blender, cover, and blend at high speed until smooth. Occasionally scrape sides of blender with rubber spatula. Pour into saucepan and add remaining broth. Simmer 5 minutes. Cool slightly.

Combine egg yolks and cream with 1 cup of hot broth and slowly stir into soup. Add food coloring, if desired. Simmer, without boiling, for 2 minutes while beating constantly. Chill at least 2 hours. Serve hot (do not boil) or cold, garnished with watercress leaves.

Entrées

To simplify your menu-planning, try planning dinners and lunches a week in advance, based on your entrée. A meat day, a seafood day, an egg day, a poultry day, a casserole day, and, for variety, try a menu focused around a hearty soup, salad, or all-vegetable day. For economy's sake do your planning the night the supermarket advertising appears in your area and work out menus according to the best buys for the week ahead. When you prepare dishes from this book that keep well in the freezer, such as blanquette of veal, coq au vin or beef burgundy, and their main ingredients are on sale that week, prepare a double batch and freeze it ahead. You'll save both time and money!

If there are leftovers, they can provide the basis for a lunch next day (if anyone is home these days to eat lunch), and, if not, they could become the basis for a nutritious soup you improvise.

The entrées we will cover in the pages ahead include beef, game, ham, lamb, pork, poultry, seafood, variety meats and veal, all prepared deliciously but in the very low carbohydrate way. Further on in this book you will find a variety of egg and vegetable dishes for the nights you want to rely on those as your mainstay.

BEEF

SAMPLE BEEF MENUS

Prosciutto and melon*
Boeuf Bourguignon
Caesar salad*
Frozen Grand Marnier mousse*

Cream of watercress soup*
Filet mignon, Cordon Bleu
Fresh asparagus
Céleri rémoulade*
Coupe de luxe*

Lobster cocktail*
Fillet of beef Béarnaise
Spinach soufflé*
Tossed green salad
Daiquiri lime parfait*

Chopped chicken livers*
Roast fillet of beef périgueux
Green beans with mushrooms*
Bibb lettuce salad
Fresh strawberries and mandarin
    orange sections with sour
    cream

Onion soup*
Beef fondue
Cucumber and onion salad*
Cheese fondue with green
    apples*

Eggs à la Russe*
Stuffed green peppers
Caesar salad*
Coffee Bavarian cream*

Cold tomato soup*
Burgundy hamburgers
Fresh broccoli
Cucumber and onion salad*
Peaches royale*

Prosciutto and melon*
London broil
Fresh asparagus
Caesar salad*
Fresh fruit and cheese*

Petite marmite*
*Oxtail ragout**
Fresh green beans
Sliced mushroom salad*
Sliced fresh peaches with rum
   custard sauce*

Cherrystone clams on the half
   shell with lemon wedge
*Rolled roast beef, Burgundy**
Baked stuffed tomato*
Tossed green salad
Fresh blueberries and sliced
   peaches with gervaise sauce*

Oysters casino*
*Beef roulades**
Mushrooms under glass*
Broccoli salad*
Persian melon with lemon
   wedge

Pâté de foie gras
*Sauerbraten**
Cauliflower au gratin*
Crisp fresh spinach salad
Coffee Bavarian cream*

Escargots*
*Steak au poivre, flambé**
Asparagus with Hollandaise*
Stuffed mushrooms Parmigiana*
Tossed green salad
Fresh fruit and cheese*

Shrimp cocktail with lemon
   wedges
*Broiled steak piquant**
Sautéed mushrooms
Buttered spinach
Cole slaw*
Fresh strawberries with sabayon
   sauce*

Eggs in aspic*
*Beef Stroganoff**
Fresh asparagus
Sliced fresh mushroom salad*
Coffee Bavarian cream*

Egg-drop soup*
*Teriyaki**
Chinese snow peas*
Sliced fresh mushroom salad*
Fresh strawberries and mandarin
   orange sections with sour
   cream

Philadelphia snapper soup*
*Tournedos Héloïse**
Glazed carrots*
Tossed green salad
Dessert cheeses*

BOEUF BOURGUIGNON
MAKES 8 SERVINGS 7.6 GRAMS PER SERVING

2 cups sliced onions
2 tablespoons bacon drippings
　or vegetable oil
3 pounds lean chuck, 1-inch
　cubes
1 ½ tablespoons flour
⅛ teaspoon marjoram

⅛ teaspoon thyme
Salt and freshly ground pepper
¾ cup beef bouillon
1 ½ cups Burgundy wine
1 pound sliced fresh
　mushrooms
Chopped fresh parsley

Sauté onions in bacon drippings in large heavy casserole until tender and browned. Set aside. Brown beef cubes on all sides in same casserole and sprinkle with flour, marjoram, thyme, salt, and pepper. Stir in bouillon, scraping sides and bottom of the casserole. Add wine.

Cover and simmer over very low heat (or transfer casserole to preheated 250° F. oven) for 3 hours.

Add more liquid if necessary—one part bouillon to two parts wine. Stir in onions and mushrooms and simmer 1 hour or until meat is tender when tested with a fork. Sprinkle with parsley and serve piping hot from the casserole.

FILET MIGNON, CORDON BLEU
MAKES 8 SERVINGS .5 GRAM PER SERVING

8 8-ounce filet mignon,
　1 ½-inches thick
16 thin slices prosciutto ham

16 thin slices Gruyère cheese
½ cup Béarnaise sauce (see
　Sauces)

Preheat broiler and broil filets 1 minute on each side. Remove from broiler. Slice each filet horizontally three-fourths of the way across. Fill opening with two slices of ham and two slices of cheese in alternating layers. Return filet to broiler for additional 2 minutes per side (rare) to 5 minutes per side (well done). Pour 1 tablespoon of Béarnaise sauce over each filet and broil again for a few seconds. Serve immediately.

FILLET OF BEEF BÉARNAISE
MAKES 8 SERVINGS 5.6 GRAMS PER SERVING

8 8-ounce fillets of beef
8 ¼-inch slices Burmuda
   onion
1 teaspoon sweet basil

8 thick slices beefsteak
   tomatoes
1¾ cups Béarnaise sauce (see
   Sauces)

Preheat broiler. Broil steaks to preferred doneness. Broil onion slices sprinkled with sweet basil for 5 minutes. Place steaks on heated platter and top each with broiled onion and tomato slice. Cover liberally with Béarnaise sauce and serve piping hot.

ROAST FILLET OF BEEF PÉRIGUEUX
MAKES 8 SERVINGS 3.1 GRAMS PER SERVING

1 4-pound beef tenderloin
2 tablespoons butter or
   margarine
2 tablespoons vegetable oil
Salt and freshly ground pepper

3 cups *sauce périgueux*
   (see *Sauces*)
Goose liver pâté, sliced 1-inch
   square
Sliced truffles
Watercress

Preheat oven to 300° F.

Sear meat in butter and oil in heavy skillet until well browned on all sides. Transfer to roasting pan and sprinkle with salt and pepper. Prepare *sauce périgueux* and strain it over meat. Roast meat 1 hour and 20 minutes or until desired doneness (thermometer—140° for rare, 150° for medium rare, 160° for medium). Garnish roast with pâte, sliced truffles, and watercress. Serve hot sauce separately.

BEEF FONDUE
MAKES 8 SERVINGS   2.8 GRAMS PER SERVING

Peanut oil
1-inch heel of bread or raw
  potato

4 pounds very lean beef fillet,
  1-inch cubes

Fill heavy fondue pot half full of oil. Start to heat oil on stove. When piping hot transfer fondue pot to warming stand over regulated heat. Put bread in simmering oil to prevent splattering when meat is immersed. At dinner table guests pierce raw meat with fondue forks or long wooden skewers and submerge it in hot oil and cook meat to desired doneness.

Serve beef fondue with choice of three or four of following sauces:

Béarnaise sauce	.3 gram per tablespoon
Chopped scallions	.6 gram per tablespoon
Curry-dill dip	.3 gram per tablespoon
Dresden sauce	.5 gram per tablespoon
Epicurean sauce	.3 gram per tablespoon
Mustard sauce	.5 gram per tablespoon
Rémoulade sauce	.2 gram per tablespoon
Sauce verte	.2 gram per tablespoon
Tartar sauce	.3 gram per tablespoon

STUFFED GREEN PEPPERS

MAKES 8 SERVINGS   8.3 GRAMS PER SERVING

8 green peppers
½ cup chopped onions
½ teaspoon minced garlic
1 tablespoon olive or
   vegetable oil
2 pounds ground lean beef
1½ cups peeled, diced
   tomatoes, fresh or canned
½ pound fresh mushrooms,
   sliced
1 cup diced mozzarella
   cheese

2 teaspoons Worcestershire
   sauce
2 tablespoons chopped fresh
   parsley
½ teaspoon celery salt
¼ teaspoon basil or chervil
Salt and freshly ground pepper
½ cup V-8 juice
3 tablespoons freshly ground
   Parmesan cheese

Cut peppers in half lengthwise and remove seeds and ribs. Drop peppers into boiling salted water, turn heat off, and set aside for 5 minutes. Drain.

Sauté onions and garlic in oil until tender. Stir in beef and sauté until evenly browned. Drain tomatoes, combining juice with V-8 juice, and stir into skillet along with remaining ingredients (except juices and Parmesan cheese). Cool slightly. Stuff peppers with meat mixture and set close together in greased baking dish. Pour tomato juices around them and sprinkle each with Parmesan cheese.

Preheat oven to 350° F. and bake peppers 40 minutes or until tender. Occasionally baste with tomato juice and add more V-8 juice to pan, if necessary.

BURGUNDY HAMBURGERS
MAKES 8 SERVINGS   .2 GRAM PER SERVING

2½ pounds freshly ground lean
    round steak
2 3-ounce cans deviled or
    Smithfield ham spread
½ pound Roquefort or bleu
    cheese

1 cup Burgundy wine
2 tablespoons butter or
    margarine
Salt and freshly ground pepper

Combine ground round steak with ham spread and divide into eight equal portions. Mold meat completely around cheese cut into 1¼-inch squares ½-inch thick. Pour wine over hamburgers, cover, and refrigerate for 3 hours, turning once. Drain and reserve wine.

Preheat broiler. Melt butter in shallow baking pan and broil hamburgers 2 inches from heat for approximately 4 minutes per side (rare) to 6 minutes per side (well done). Remove hamburgers to heated platter. Stir wine into pan, scrape sides and bottom, bring to a boil, and reduce to ½ cup. Season sauce with salt and pepper and pour it over hamburgers.

LONDON BROIL
MAKES 8 SERVINGS   1.0 GRAM PER SERVING

1 4-pound lean top round steak
    (London broil)
1 cup boiling water
¼ cup red wine vinegar
2 tablespoons vegetable oil
1 tablespoon tomato paste
¼ teaspoon minced garlic

2 tablespoons chopped onion
½ crumbled bay leaf
¼ teaspoon crushed dried
    bouquet garni
¼ teaspoon cracked pepper-
    corns
1 teaspoon *salt*

Remove all fat from steak and thoroughly score. Combine remaining ingredients and pour over steak. Cover and marinate at room temperature 4 hours or overnight in refrigerator. Turn meat several times.

Preheat broiler. Drain and reserve marinade. Broil steak quickly, 7 minutes per side, basting frequently with marinade to prevent charring. To serve, thinly slice meat diagonally across grain and place on heated platter. Strain and heat marinade. Spoon some sauce over slices and serve the rest separately.

OXTAIL RAGOÛT

MAKES 8 SERVINGS 7.0 GRAMS PER SERVING

4 oxtails, skinned and cut up
Seasoned flour
1 cup chopped celery
1 cup chopped onions
1 cup chopped peeled carrots
1 teaspoon minced garlic
2 tablespoons bacon drippings
  or vegetable oil
1 cup beef bouillon
1 cup dry red wine
2 cups Italian plum tomatoes,
  peeled and chopped

¼ cup chopped fresh parsley
½ teaspoon thyme
1 bay leaf
¼ teaspoon freshly grated
  nutmeg
½ pound sliced fresh
  mushrooms
½ cup Madeira wine
Salt and freshly ground pepper
Chopped fresh parsley
3 tablespoons warm brandy

Preheat oven to 350° F.

Wash and thoroughly dry pieces of oxtail. Dredge with seasoned flour. Brown oxtail, celery, onions, carrots, and garlic in bacon drippings in heavy casserole about 10 minutes. Stir in bouillon and scrape sides and bottom of casserole. Add wine, tomatoes, parsley, thyme, and bay leaf. Bring to a boil, cover, and transfer to preheated 350° oven to cook for 2 hours.

Set oxtail aside. Strain liquid and press cooked vegetables through sieve. Return all to casserole and bring to a boil. Add nutmeg, mushrooms, and Madeira wine. Lower heat and sim-

mer 30 minutes longer. Season with salt and pepper, if needed.
Sprinkle with additional chopped parsley and serve from deep,
heated platter. Ignite warm brandy and sprinkle flaming liquor
over ragoût.

ROLLED ROAST BEEF, BURGUNDY
MAKES 8 SERVINGS   1.0 GRAM PER SERVING

1 6-pound rolled cross rib roast	2 cups Burgundy or mountain
2 tablespoons butter or	red wine
margarine	Salt
2 tablespoons vegetable oil	10 peppercorns, crushed
½ cup chopped onions	1 bay leaf
½ cup chopped leeks	¼ teaspoon marjoram
½ cup chopped peeled carrots	½ teaspoon thyme
¼ teaspoon crushed garlic	2 tablespoons heated cognac

Brown roast on all sides in butter and oil in Dutch oven.
Remove meat and set aside. Sauté onions, leeks, carrots, and
garlic in Dutch oven until brown. Place roast on top of vegetables. Add wine combined with spices. Ignite cognac and
pour over roast.

Preheat oven to 325° F. Cover and bake until meat is tender,
about 4 hours. Add more wine, if necessary. Place roast on
heated platter. Strain and bring sauce to a boil and reduce to
1 cup. Pour sauce over roast and serve piping hot.

BEEF ROULADES
MAKES 8 SERVINGS   5.0 GRAMS PER SERVING

6 slices bacon	2 tablespoons flour
1 cup minced onions	½ teaspoon crushed dried
4 pounds lean top round steak,	*bouquet garni* for beef
½ inch thick	3 cups strong beef bouillon
2 tablespoons prepared hot	2 tablespoons sherry
mustard	Fresh parsley
Salt and freshly ground pepper	

Partially cook bacon in Dutch oven, drain, chop, and combine with onions. Reserve 1 tablespoon of bacon drippings in Dutch oven. Pound steaks with wooden mallet or rolling pin to ¼-inch thickness and spread one side with mustard. Lightly salt and pepper both sides. Cut meat into 3- by 4-inch rectangles. Spread bacon-onion mixture on meat, roll, and secure with skewer or string. Brown rolled beef in bacon drippings and set aside. Sprinkle flour and *bouquet garni* into Dutch oven and slowly stir in bouillon, scraping sides and bottom of oven.

Preheat oven to 250° F. Return meat to Dutch oven, cover, and bake 1½ hours, turning meat once. Place roulades on heated platter and discard skewers or string. Add sherry to Dutch oven, bring to a rapid boil, and reduce to 2 cups. Pour sauce over roulades and serve garnished with parsley.

SAUERBRATEN
MAKES 8 SERVINGS   6.0 GRAMS PER SERVING

2½ cups dry red wine	¼ teaspoon allspice
1½ cups red wine vinegar	1 teaspoon dry mustard
1½ cups sliced onions	1 teaspoon salt
½ cup sliced peeled carrots	10 peppercorns
½ cup chopped celery tops with leaves	4- to 5-pound eye of the round roast
1 garlic clove, halved	3 tablespoons bacon drippings
2 bay leaves	
6 whole cloves	6 crumbled gingersnaps
½ teaspoon thyme	1 cup sour cream

Combine all ingredients (except roast, bacon drippings, gingersnaps, and sour cream) and bring to a rapid boil. Pour marinade over roast in a large enamel kettle or bowl and cover with cheesecloth. Marinate for 4 days at room temperature or 1 week in refrigerator, turning meat twice a day.

Remove meat from marinade, dry with paper towels, and

reserve marinade. Sear meat on all sides in the bacon drippings in large Dutch oven. Pour marinade over meat, add ginger-snaps, cover, and simmer 3 or 4 hours or until meat is tender when tested with a fork. Thinly slice meat diagonally across grain and arrange on heated platter. Strain marinade, stir in sour cream, and reheat without boiling. Spoon some of sauce over slices and serve the rest separately.

STEAK AU POIVRE, FLAMBÉ
MAKES 8 SERVINGS .3 GRAM PER SERVING

8 8-ounce fillets of beef, 1-inch thick
4 tablespoons cracked peppercorns
Salt

¼ cup heated cognac
1 tablespoon heavy cream
8 tablespoons maître d'hôtel butter (see *Sauces*)

Press peppercorns into both sides of fillets. Set aside for 30 minutes or longer. Sprinkle salt lightly over bottom of heavy skillet. When salt begins to brown over high heat, sear steaks until well browned on both sides. Continue to cook steaks over moderate heat for 3 or 4 minutes per side, depending on desired doneness. Transfer fillets to heated platter and keep warm. Ignite cognac and pour it into skillet. Rotate skillet until flame dies. Return skillet to low heat, add cream, stir, and scrape sides and bottom of pan. Pour sauce over fillets and serve garnished with squares of maître d'hôtel butter.

BROILED STEAK PIQUANTE
MAKES 8 SERVINGS 2.1 GRAMS PER SERVING

8 8-ounce lean steaks
1 cup Roquefort or blue cheese
3 tablespoons butter or margarine
4 tablespoons grated onions

½ cup Madeira wine
2 tablespoons tomato purée
Dash Tabasco
Salt and freshly ground pepper

Preheat broiler.

Broil steaks to preferred doneness. Place on ovenproof serving platter. Blend remaining ingredients in electric blender until smooth. Spread evenly over each broiled steak and return steaks to broiler for 10 seconds. Serve immediately.

BEEF STROGANOFF

MAKES 8 SERVINGS   7.3 GRAMS PER SERVING

3 pounds lean beef tenderloin, ¼-inch thick
Salt and freshly ground pepper
¾ pound fresh mushrooms, sliced
3 tablespoons butter or margarine

¾ cup thinly sliced onions
2 tablespoons flour
2 cups beef bouillon
3 tablespoons dry sherry
2 tablespoons tomato paste
1 tablespoon dry mustard
⅔ cup sour cream

Cut beef into 3-by-¾-inch strips and sprinkle lightly with salt and pepper. Set aside for 2 hours at room temperature. Sauté mushrooms in butter for 3 minutes or until tender. Remove and set aside. Sauté onions in same skillet until tender and browned. Remove and set aside. Sear sliced beef in same skillet until just rare. Remove and set aside.

Brown flour in same skillet. Slowly add bouillon and stir until smooth. Stir in sherry, tomato paste, and mustard. Stir in mushrooms, onions, and meat and simmer, without boiling, for 20 minutes. At serving time, add sour cream, stir, and simmer, without boiling, for 5 minutes or until piping hot.

TERIYAKI

MAKES 8 SERVINGS   4.0 GRAMS PER SERVING

3 pounds sirloin steak, 1-inch thick
½ cup soy sauce
½ cup dry sherry

1 teaspoon grated fresh or ½ teaspoon ground ginger
½ teaspoon minced garlic
1 tablespoon grated onion
1 tablespoon sugar

Trim steak of all fat and slice diagonally across grain ⅛-inch thick. Combine remaining ingredients with beef slices and marinate 1 to 2 hours.

Preheat broiler. Thread meat on metal or bamboo skewers accordion style and broil 30 seconds over wire rack in broiler pan. Strain marinade, heat, and serve in individual bowls to use as dip for teriyaki.

TOURNEDOS HÉLOÏSE
MAKES 8 SERVINGS 7.1 GRAMS PER SERVING

Salt
8 tournedos of beef, 1-inch
  thick
8 large artichoke bottoms
2 tablespoons butter or
  margarine

⅛ teaspoon Bovril
1 tablespoon hot water
½ cup Madeira wine
8 slices pâté de foie gras
8 slices truffles

Sprinkle salt lightly over bottom of heavy skillet and place over high heat. Sear steaks until well browned on both sides. Continue to cook steaks over moderate heat for 3 or 4 minutes per side, depending on desired doneness. Heat artichoke bottoms in butter and arrange on heated platter. Place tournedo on top of each artichoke bottom and keep warm.

Stir Bovril, water, and wine into skillet and scrape sides and bottom of pan. Simmer 3 minutes and pour over tournedos. Garnish each tournedo with slice of pâté topped by slice of truffle.

GAME

~

SAMPLE GAME MENUS

Eggs à la Russe*
*Civet of Hare**
Braised Belgian endive*
Wilted spinach salad*
Strawberries Romanoff*

Petite marmite*
*Roast pheasant with Madeira
    sauce**
Broiled tomatoes*
Tossed green salad
Coupe de luxe*

Moules ravigote*
*Rock Cornish game hen with
    grape stuffing**
Spinach soufflé*
Sliced mushroom salad*
Cantaloupe with Cheddar cheese

Gazpacho*
*Rock Cornish game hen with
    liver and ham stuffing**
Cauliflower au gratin*
Fresh crisp spinach salad
Fresh strawberries and mandarin
    orange sections with sour
    cream

Shrimp cocktail*
*Rock Cornish game hen with
    sausage stuffing**
Fresh asparagus
Tossed green salad
Fresh fruit and cheese*

Jellied chicken consommé
*Venison sauté**
Brussels sprouts sauté*
Cole slaw*
Coupe de luxe*

52

Petite marmite*
Brandied wild duck
Spinach soufflé*
Endive salad
Fresh fruit and cheese*

CIVET OF HARE

MAKES 8 SERVINGS   5.7 GRAMS PER SERVING

2 young rabbits, cut into serving pieces
2 cups Burgundy wine
½ teaspoon minced garlic
2 tablespoons minced shallots
1 tablespoon chopped fresh parsley
⅛ teaspoon thyme
1 bay leaf
1 cup diced salt pork

16 small pearl onions
2 tablespoons flour
1 cup beef bouillon
½ pound fresh mushrooms
2 tablespoons prepared hot mustard (Dijon or Düsseldorf)
Salt and freshly ground pepper
Parsley

Cover pieces of rabbit with combination of wine, garlic, shallots, parsley, thyme, and bay leaf. Marinate overnight in refrigerator. Cover salt pork with water and boil 5 minutes. Drain and sauté in heavy casserole until evenly browned. Set aside. Brown onions in casserole and set aside. Dry rabbit pieces, sprinkle with flour, and brown on all sides in casserole. Discard excess drippings. Pour marinade and bouillon over rabbit, bring to a boil, cover, and simmer 45 minutes.

Discard bay leaf. Add salt pork, onions, and mushrooms. Cover and continue to cook slowly 30 minutes or until meat is tender and comes easily away from bone. Transfer rabbit and vegetables to heated platter. Blend mustard with 1 cup of sauce and stir into casserole. Scrape sides and bottom of pan. Add salt and pepper, if needed. Pour some sauce over rabbit and garnish with parsley. Serve remaining sauce separately.

ROAST PHEASANT WITH MADEIRA SAUCE
MAKES 8 SERVINGS   4.9 GRAMS PER SERVING

3   2½- to 3-pound pheasants
Lemon juice
Brandy
1   cup diced celery with leaves
1   cup diced peeled carrots
1   cup diced onions
2   tablespoons butter or
    margarine
1   cup Madeira wine

2   tart apples, peeled and
    quartered
Salt and freshly ground pepper
6   slices of bacon
1   cup consommé
2   tablespoons flour
2   tablespoons softened butter
    or margarine
3   cooked pheasant livers, finely
    chopped

Rub inside and outside of pheasants with lemon juice and again with brandy. Sauté celery, carrots, and onions in butter for 5 minutes. Add wine, cover, and cook 2 minutes. Strain, reserving liquid, and set vegetables aside to cool. Combine vegetables with apple quarters and spoon equal portions into cavity of each pheasant. Place pheasants, breast side up, on a rack in roasting pan. Pour Madeira sauce over birds. Sprinkle with salt and pepper. Cover breasts with strips of bacon. Cover each pheasant with butter-soaked cheesecloth.

Preheat oven to 350° F. Roast 30 minutes per pound of one pheasant or until juices run clear when thigh joint is pricked. Baste frequently with pan juices. Discard cheesecloth, bacon, vegetables, and apples. Place pheasants on heated platter. Add consommé to roasting pan and stir over moderate heat. Scrape bottom and sides of pan. Blend flour with softened butter and stir into gravy. Add chopped livers and simmer 2 minutes or until gravy thickens slightly. Serve gravy separately.

᠁

ROCK CORNISH GAME HEN

MAKES 8 SERVINGS   1.7 GRAMS PER SERVING

8 Rock Cornish game hens
1 lemon, halved
Salt and freshly ground pepper
1½ tablespoons fresh lemon
    juice
8 slices of bacon, halved

¼ pound butter or margarine
¼ cup warm cognac
1 teaspoon minced shallots
2 cups beef bouillon
½ cup Madeira wine

Rub inside of each game hen with freshly cut lemon, salt, and pepper. Sprinkle outside with lemon juice, salt, and pepper. Stuff hens with one of stuffings below. Tie legs together over tail. Brown birds in butter and arrange, breast side up, on a rack in large roasting pan. Ignite warmed cognac and pour over each bird. Lay bacon across each bird to cover wing tips and legs.

Preheat oven to 400° F. Roast 40 to 45 minutes (basting frequently) or until juices run clear when thigh joint is pricked. Remove string from legs and place hens on heated platter. Discard all but 2 tablespoons of drippings from roasting pan. Add shallots and sauté until tender. Stir in bouillon and wine and scrape sides and bottom of pan. Bring to a boil and reduce sauce to 1 cup. Spoon sauce over each bird and serve.

Each of the following three recipes will stuff eight game hens (Rock Cornish, squab, quail, or partridge), eight 1-pound chickens, or three pheasants.

GRAPE STUFFING

MAKES 3½ CUPS   4.1 GRAMS PER SERVING

½ pound fresh mushrooms,
    finely chopped
2 tablespoons butter or
    margarine

32 white seedless grapes
3 tablespoons pâté de foie gras

Sauté mushrooms in butter. Spoon equal portion into cavity of each bird along with four grapes and a teaspoon of pâté.

LIVER AND HAM STUFFING

MAKES 3½ CUPS   3.0 GRAMS PER SERVING

8 chicken or game hen livers
2 tablespoons butter or
  margarine
½ pound fresh mushrooms,
  chopped

¾ cup chopped cooked ham
¼ cup coarsely chopped
  pistachio nuts

Sauté livers in butter until just tender. Chop. Sauté mushrooms in same skillet for 2 minutes. Combine all ingredients and loosely stuff birds.

SAUSAGE STUFFING

MAKES 3 CUPS   3.0 GRAMS PER SERVING

1 pound cooked pork sausage
  meat
1 egg, beaten
¼ cup minced fresh parsley

¼ cup minced onions
¼ cup coarsely chopped
  pistachio nuts

Combine all ingredients and spoon equal portions into cavity of each bird.

VENISON SAUTÉ

MAKES 8 SERVINGS 3.6 GRAMS PER SERVING

8 fillets or loin chops of
  venison, ½- to ¾-inch thick
2 cups dry red wine
1 cup wine vinegar
½ cup water
1 cup chopped onions
1 tablespoon chopped
  shallots
½ cup chopped peeled carrots
½ teaspoon chopped garlic
2 bay leaves
6 peppercorns, crushed
4 tablespoons vegetable oil
1½ cups sour cream
Salt and freshly ground pepper

Combine all ingredients (except oil, sour cream, salt, and pepper) in large glass or enamel casserole. Cover and refrigerate for 24 hours, turning once or twice. Wipe meat dry. Strain and reserve marinade for gravy. Flatten fillets with wooden mallet or rolling pin. Sauté fillets in oil over high heat for not more than 1 minute per side. (Sauté venison chops over medium-high heat for 4 minutes per side.) Remove meat to heated platter.

Bring strained marinade to a boil and reduce to 1 cup. Add sour cream, stir, and heat without boiling. Add salt and pepper, if needed. Serve gravy separately.

BRANDIED WILD DUCK

MAKES 8 SERVINGS 2.7 GRAMS PER SERVING

2 cups chicken broth
1 cup chopped onions
2 tablespoons chopped fresh
  parsley
1 teaspoon thyme
1 bay leaf
1 tablespoon grated orange
  rind
Salt and freshly ground pepper
1 cup brandy
4 wild ducks, each cut into
  8 pieces
3 tablespoons bacon drippings
½ teaspoon chopped garlic
1 pound fresh mushrooms,
  sliced

Simmer chicken broth, onions, parsley, thyme, bay leaf, orange rind, salt, and pepper 10 minutes and cool. Combine with brandy and pour over ducks in a large bowl. Marinate for 5 hours at room temperature. Set duck pieces aside. Strain marinade and reserve.

Evenly brown duck pieces in bacon drippings combined with garlic in Dutch oven for 20 minutes. Add mushrooms and strained marinade. Cover and simmer for 1½ hours or until duck is tender when tested with a fork. Transfer duck to heated platter. Bring liquid in Dutch oven to a rapid boil. Stir and scrape sides and bottom of pan, until gravy is slightly reduced and thickened. Pour gravy over duck and serve piping hot.

HAM

SAMPLE HAM MENUS

Pâté de foie gras
Chou farci*
Cucumber and onion salad*
Coffee Bavarian cream*

Crab cocktail with lemon wedge
Baked ham with cider glaze*
Fresh asparagus
Fresh fruit compote with
    gervaise sauce*

Jellied chicken consommé
*Baked ham with cranberry ham
    glaze**
Cauliflower au gratin*
Crisp fresh spinach salad
Petit pot de creme*

Eggs à la Russe*
*Baked ham with grenadine
    glaze**
Stuffed zucchini*
Bibb lettuce salad
Strawberries Romanoff*

Petite marmite*
Baked ham with rum glaze*
Spinach soufflé*
Tossed green salad
Persian melon with lemon wedge

Oysters casino*
Baked ham in Madeira*
Fresh asparagus
Cole slaw*
Frozen Grand Marnier mousse*

Lobster cocktail with lemon
    wedge
Baked ham steak in wine sauce*
Broiled tomato*
Asparagus vinaigrette*
Coeur à la crème*

CHOU FARCI—STUFFED CABBAGE

MAKES 8 SERVINGS   9.7 GRAMS PER SERVING

1 large Savoy cabbage, 8 inches in diameter	¼ cup chopped fresh parsley
1 pound sausage meat	1 egg, lightly beaten
1½ cups diced cooked ham	Salt and freshly ground pepper
½ cup chopped onions	5 thick slices bacon, halved
¼ teaspoon minced garlic	½ cup sliced onions
¾ cup cooked rice	½ cup sliced peeled carrots
¼ teaspoon sage	2 cups beef bouillon
½ teaspoon caraway seeds	1 can stewed tomatoes

Discard tough outer leaves of cabbage and remove center core. Carefully peel off leaves and drop into boiling salted water. Boil 3 minutes or until they bend easily. Drain. Sauté sausage meat 5 minutes and break it up with fork. Set aside. Brown diced ham, onions, and garlic in same skillet. Drain well. Combine all with rice, sage, caraway seeds, parsley, egg, salt, and pepper.

Line a 2-quart bowl with large double thickness of cheese-cloth. Add five largest cabbage leaves, slightly overlapping, with stem ends up. Evenly spread a quarter of meat stuffing toward, but not up to, ends of leaves. Place four more leaves as before and spread with another quarter of stuffing. Repeat, making two more layers of leaves and stuffing. Bring edges of cheesecloth together and tie securely, reshaping cabbage.

Preheat oven to 350° F. Line large, heavy casserole with half of bacon and spread sliced onions and carrots evenly over them. Add stuffed cabbage, tied side down, and pour in bouillon and tomatoes. Place remaining strips of bacon over cabbage, cover, and bake for 2½ hours. Remove cabbage to heated platter and discard cheesecloth. Dry slices of bacon, brown lightly, chop, and sprinkle over chou farci. Strain cooking liquid and serve separately.

GLAZED BAKED HAM
MAKES 8 OR MORE SERVINGS   (UNGLAZED HAM 0 GRAMS)

1 8- to 10-pound tenderized, precooked or canned ham	30 to 40 whole cloves Ham glaze (see below)

Preheat oven to 325° F. Remove rind and excess fat from ham. Score fat ¼ inch deep diagonally in 1-inch diamonds. Stud each diamond with a clove. Insert meat thermometer into ham, away from bone. Bake tenderized ham on a rack 20 to 25 minutes per pound or until meat thermometer reads 160° F. Bake precooked or canned ham on a rack 15 to 20 minutes per pound or until meat thermometer reads 130° F. When ham is done, remove from oven and spread with one of glazes below. Increase oven heat to 400° F. Return ham to oven and bake 30 minutes longer or until ham is well glazed. Baste occasionally.

Each of following four recipes will glaze an 8- to 10-pound baked ham or can be brushed onto individual baked ham steaks.

CIDER HAM GLAZE
MAKES 5.6 GRAMS PER SERVING

1 cup cider	Freshly grated nutmeg
2 tablespoons red currant jelly	1 teaspoon dry mustard
½ teaspoon ground cinnamon	

Combine all ingredients and heat until jelly melts.

CRANBERRY HAM GLAZE
MAKES 6.9 GRAMS PER SERVING

½ cup whole berry cranberry
   sauce
¼ cup cranberry juice

2 tablespoons grated orange
   rind
1 teaspoon dry mustard

Combine all ingredients and heat until cranberry sauce melts.

GRENADINE HAM GLAZE
MAKES 6.1 GRAMS PER SERVING

½ cup grenadine syrup
1 teaspoon allspice

Freshly ground pepper

Combine all ingredients into a smooth mixture.

RUM HAM GLAZE
MAKES 6.4 GRAMS PER SERVING

2 tablespoons Myers's rum
5 tablespoons dark brown
   sugar, packed

Freshly grated nutmeg
1 teaspoon dry mustard

Combine all ingredients into smooth mixture.

BAKED HAM IN MADEIRA

MAKES 8 OR MORE SERVINGS 6.1 GRAMS PER SERVING

1 8- to 10-pound precooked ham
1 cup Madeira wine
2 cups beef bouillon
½ teaspoon thyme
1 bay leaf
¼ cup sifted confectioners' sugar
1 tablespoon arrowroot
3 chopped canned truffles and juice
3 tablespoons softened butter or margarine
Watercress or fresh parsley

Preheat oven to 325° F. Remove rind and excess fat from ham and insert meat thermometer into ham, away from bone. Place on a rack in roasting pan. Combine wine and bouillon and pour over ham. Sprinkle with thyme and fasten bay leaf to ham with toothpick. Cover and bake 1½ hours, basting every ½ hour. Discard bay leaf.

Sprinkle ham with sugar and continue to bake 30 minutes or until meat thermometer reads 130° F. Place ham on heated platter. Skim excess fat from cooking liquid, bring to a rapid boil, and reduce to 2 cups. Stir in arrowroot, dissolved in truffle juice, and truffles and simmer 5 minutes. Add butter and stir until melted. Serve sauce separately and garnish ham with watercress or parsley.

BAKED HAM STEAKS IN WINE SAUCE

MAKES 8 SERVINGS 4.5 GRAMS PER SERVING

4 12-ounce baked ham steaks
1½ teaspoons dry mustard
3 tablespoons butter or margarine
1 pound fresh mushrooms, sliced
1 teaspoon fresh lemon juice
2 tablespoons chopped onions
1 cup dry white wine
1 tablespoon flour
2 egg yolks, lightly beaten
1 cup cream
Freshly ground white pepper
Watercress or fresh parsley

Trim most of fat from ham steaks and rub both sides with mustard. Brown steaks in butter on each side and set aside. Sauté mushrooms in same skillet for 2 minutes, sprinkle with lemon juice, remove, and set aside. Sauté onions until tender and set aside. Stir wine into skillet. Return steaks to skillet, mounding mushrooms and onions on top. Cover and simmer 1 hour. Remove steaks, mushrooms, and onions to heated platter.

Bring liquid in skillet to a rapid boil and reduce to ¼ cup. Combine flour, egg yolks, and cream and stir into reduced liquid. Heat, without boiling, and stir until sauce thickens. Season with pepper. Pour sauce over steaks and garnish with watercress or parsley.

LAMB

SAMPLE LAMB MENUS

Avgolemono soup*
*Crown roast of lamb with moussaka**
Greek salad*
Fresh fruit and cheese*

Eggs à la Russe*
*Glazed leg of lamb**
Zucchini and tomatoes*
Endive and watercress salad
Coupe de luxe*

Shrimp cocktail with lemon
   wedge
*Lamb curry**
Condiments*
Fresh asparagus
Endive salad
Daiquiri lime parfait*

Caviar Madrilène*
*Shish kebab**
Fresh broccoli
Cole slaw*
Strawberries Romanoff*

Jellied chicken consommé with
   lemon wedges
*Dolmas with lemon sauce**
Broiled tomatoes*
Greek salad*
Honeydew melon

Moules ravigote*
*Stuffed leg of lamb**
Broiled tomatoes*
Crisp spinach salad
Coffee Bavarian cream*

CROWN ROAST OF LAMB WITH MOUSSAKA
MAKES 8 SERVINGS   6.6 GRAMS PER SERVING

1 16-chop crown roast of lamb
Fresh lemon juice
Salt and freshly ground pepper
2 medium eggplants, ½-inch slices
3 tablespoons melted butter or margarine
1 pound ground lamb or beef
½ cup chopped onions
¼ teaspoon minced garlic
2½ cups peeled, diced Italian tomatoes, fresh or canned

½ cup dry red wine
¼ cup chopped fresh parsley
¼ teaspoon thyme
½ teaspoon salt
⅛ teaspoon cinnamon
2 eggs, lightly beaten
1 cup freshly grated imported Parmesan cheese
Freshly grated nutmeg
Paper frills

Preheat oven to 350° F.

Have butcher prepare a crown roast of lamb and remove excess fat. Rub all surfaces with lemon juice and sprinkle with salt and pepper. Cover tips of chops with aluminum foil to prevent charring. Insert meat thermometer into meat away from bone. Brush slices of eggplant with melted butter and sprinkle lightly with salt. Broil, about 4 inches from heat, for 4 minutes on each side or until golden brown. Set aside. Sauté ground meat with onions and garlic in remaining butter. Stir until meat is evenly browned. Add tomatoes, wine, parsley, thyme, and salt and simmer about 5 minutes or until liquid almost disappears. Cool slightly. Stir in cinnamon, eggs, and half of Parmesan cheese. Arrange alternating layers of eggplant and meat sauce sprinkled with nutmeg in a buttered casserole. End with a layer of eggplant sprinkled with nutmeg and remaining cheese.

Bake roast on rack for 1 hour 20 minutes or until thermometer reads 175° F. At same time, bake moussaka for 45 minutes or until nicely browned. Remove moussaka from oven and set aside for 30 minutes or longer. Place roast on deep heated platter. Discard aluminum foil and cover tips of chops with paper frills. Spoon moussaka into center and around base of roast and serve.

LAMB CURRY
MAKES 8 SERVINGS   6.3 GRAMS PER SERVING

1 cup chopped onions
¼ teaspoon minced garlic
2 tablespoons butter or margarine
2 tablespoons vegetable oil
3 pounds lean lamb shoulder, 1-inch cubes
1 cup diced peeled tart apples
2 to 3 tablespoons curry powder

1 teaspoon ground ginger
½ teaspoon fresh or ¼ teaspoon dried mint leaves
¼ teaspoon ground cloves
1 cup bouillon
¼ cup fresh lemon juice
1 teaspoon grated lemon rind
½ teaspoon salt
⅛ teaspoon freshly ground pepper
½ cup heavy cream

Sauté onions and garlic in heavy enamel casserole in butter and oil until tender. Set aside. Brown lamb on all sides in same casserole. Add onions, garlic, and remaining ingredients (except cream). Stir, cover, and simmer slowly 1 hour. Before serving, stir in cream and heat, without boiling. Serve lamb curry with choice of 3 or 4 of following condiments served separately in small bowls:

Slivered almonds — 1.5 grams per tablespoon
Chopped crisp bacon — .1 gram per tablespoon
Chopped fresh coconut — .5 gram per tablespoon
Chopped hard-cooked eggs — .1 gram per tablespoon
Chopped onions — 1.0 gram per tablespoon
Chopped peanuts — 1.6 grams per tablespoon
Chopped fresh pineapple — 1.2 grams per tablespoon
Chopped pine nuts — .7 gram per tablespoon
Raita (see *Dips*) — .7 gram per tablespoon
Chopped scallions — .6 gram per tablespoon

DOLMAS WITH LEMON SAUCE

MAKES 8 SERVINGS   7.5 GRAMS PER SERVING

1½ pounds ground lean lamb
1 cup minced onions
¼ cup uncooked long grain
   rice
1 teaspoon chopped fresh or
   ½ teaspoon dried mint
1 teaspoon chopped fresh or
   ½ teaspoon dried dill
1 teaspoon salt

¼ teaspoon freshly ground
   pepper
½ cup water
1 pound jar grapevine leaves
1 cup strong beef bouillon
1 tablespoon butter or
   margarine
3 eggs, well beaten
½ cup fresh lemon juice

Combine meat, onions, rice, mint, dill, salt, and pepper with water and mix well. Drain jar of grapevine leaves and thoroughly wash in clear water to remove all traces of brine. Carefully separate leaves and remove thick stem portion. Place 1 tablespoon of meat mixture on underside of each perfect leaf. Fold edges over and roll tightly toward point of leaf.

Cover bottom of well-greased Dutch oven or casserole with torn imperfect or remaining leaves. Arrange rolls closely in layers, seam side down, on bed of leaves. Cover dolmas with bouillon (add more, if necessary) and dot with butter. Weigh down rolls with a heavy plate to prevent them from opening when rice puffs.

Cover casserole and simmer over low heat for 1 hour. If dry at end of hour, add 1 cup of water and simmer 5 minutes longer. Remove dolmas to heated platter. Combine eggs and lemon juice and beat well. Stir into 1 cup of cooking liquid and pour over dolmas. Dolmas may be served hot, at room temperature, or chilled (omit eggs, but sprinkle with lemon juice and chill).

GLAZED LEG OF LAMB
MAKES 8 SERVINGS   4.4 GRAMS PER SERVING

1 6- to 7-pound leg of lamb
1 garlic clove, slivered
1 tablespoon fresh or 1
   teaspoon dried mint

¼ teaspoon thyme
Salt and freshly ground pepper
6 tablespoons mint-apple jelly
¼ cup dry sherry

Cut small slits in roast and insert garlic slivers under surface of meat. Crush mint leaves, combine with thyme, and rub into meat. Cover and refrigerate overnight.

Preheat oven to 325° F. Place lamb, fat side up, on a rack in roasting pan and sprinkle with salt and pepper. Insert meat thermometer into meat away from bone. Roast 1¼ hours or until meat thermometer reads 140° F. Heat jelly and sherry until jelly melts and pour over meat. Return the roast to oven for ½ hour or until thermometer reads 170° F. Remove meat to heated platter and let stand for 20 minutes before carving. Scrape sides and bottom of roasting pan and pour pan juices over roast and serve.

SHISH KEBAB
MAKES 8 SERVINGS   4.7 GRAMS PER SERVING

1 cup dry red wine
¼ cup olive or vegetable oil
2 tablespoons grated onion
¼ teaspoon minced garlic
1 tablespoon Worcestershire
   sauce
1 crumbled bay leaf
1 teaspoon oregano

1½ teaspoons salt
Freshly ground pepper
1 5- to 6-pound leg of lamb,
   1-inch cubes
8 cherry tomatoes, halved
16 mushroom caps
Sliced bacon squares
Green pepper squares

Combine wine, oil, onions, garlic, Worcestershire sauce, and spices. Pour over lamb and top with tomatoes and mushroom caps. Weigh all down with a plate and refrigerate overnight. Drain meat, tomatoes, and mushroom caps, reserving marinade. Thread meat on individual skewers, alternating with tomatoes, mushroom caps, bacon, and green peppers. Brush with marinade.

Broil shish kebabs over a wire rack in broiler pan under high heat or over charcoal for 5 minutes on each side (about 20 to 25 minutes). Baste frequently with marinade to prevent charring. Heat remaining marinade and serve separately.

STUFFED LEG OF LAMB

MAKES 8 SERVINGS   3.7 GRAMS PER SERVING

¼ pound mushrooms, chopped
2 tablespoons chopped onions
¼ teaspoon chopped garlic
¼ pound ground lean lamb
2 tablespoons butter or margarine
¼ pound cooked lean ham, chopped
1 teaspoon chopped fresh parsley
1 tablespoon grated lemon rind
Freshly grated nutmeg
Salt and freshly ground pepper

3 egg yolks, lightly beaten
½ cup soft gluten bread cubes
1 6- to 7-pound leg of lamb, boned
2 tablespoons olive or vegetable oil
1 bay leaf
⅛ teaspoon thyme
⅛ teaspoon marjoram
2 garlic cloves, halved
2 cups chicken broth
1 cup rosé wine

Sauté mushrooms, onions, garlic, and ground lamb in butter until mushrooms are tender and lamb is evenly browned. Stir in ham, parsley, lemon rind, nutmeg, salt, and pepper. Combine egg yolks with bread cubes and toss all together. Stuff lamb cavity with stuffing and lace opening closed with skewers and string. Brown stuffed lamb in oil on all sides and transfer to Dutch oven.

Preheat oven to 325° F. Combine remaining ingredients and pour around roast. Insert meat thermometer into meat. Cover and bake 2 hours or until meat thermometer reads 170° F. Remove meat to heated platter. Strain cooking liquid, bring to a rapid boil, and reduce to 1½ cups. Serve sauce separately.

PORK

SAMPLE PORK MENUS

Senegalese soup*
*Baked pork chops**
Green beans with dill
Tossed green salad
Sliced apples and mandarin
    orange sections

Chopped chicken livers*
*Pork chops charcutière**
Beets with orange sauce*
. Bibb lettuce salad
Persian melon with cheese

Pâté de foie gras
*Pork chops and sauerkraut**
Caesar salad*
Coffee Bavarian cream*

Egg-drop soup*
*Stuffed pork chops**
Chinese snow peas*
Sliced mushroom salad*
Fresh strawberries and mandarin
    orange sections with rum cus-
    tard sauce*

Oysters Rockefeller*
Crown roast of pork with apple
    *stuffing**
Buttered spinach
Cucumber and onion salad*
Dessert cheeses*

Borscht*
*Herbed pork roast**
Green beans
Tossed green salad
Frozen Grand Marnier mousse*

Onion soup*
*Barbecued spareribs**
Fresh broccoli
Sliced mushroom salad*
Fresh fruit and cheese*

BAKED PORK CHOPS
MAKES 8 SERVINGS 3.3 GRAMS PER SERVING

16 center-cut pork chops
1 teaspoon vegetable oil
Salt and freshly ground pepper
1 cup fresh orange juice
1 teaspoon sugar
1 tablespoon freshly grated
  orange rind
¼ teaspoon freshly grated
  nutmeg
Fresh watercress

Cut off all fat and bone from chops. Brown meat on both sides in large skillet brushed with oil. Sprinkle with salt and pepper and transfer to a large casserole. Combine orange juice, sugar, orange rind, and nutmeg and pour over meat.

Preheat oven to 350° F. Cover and bake 1 hour. To serve, transfer chops to heated serving platter, spoon some sauce over each chop, and garnish with watercress.

PORK CHOPS CHARCUTIÈRE
MAKES 8 SERVINGS 3.0 GRAMS PER SERVING

16 center-cut pork chops,
  ½-inch thick
1 teaspoon vegetable oil
Salt and freshly ground pepper
2 tablespoons minced shallots
½ cup minced onions
1 tablespoon butter or
  margarine
1 teaspoon flour
¾ cup dry white wine
1 cup bouillon
1 tablespoon prepared hot
  mustard (Dijon or Düsseldorf)
3 tablespoons thinly sliced
  gherkin pickles
Chopped fresh parsley

Brown well-trimmed chops on both sides in heavy skillet brushed with oil. Sprinkle with salt and pepper and transfer to large casserole. Sauté shallots and onions in same skillet in butter until tender. Sprinkle with flour and stir in wine, bouillon, mustard, and pickles. Simmer 5 minutes and pour over chops.

Preheat oven to 350° F. Cover and bake 1 hour. To serve, transfer chops to heated serving platter, spoon some sauce over chops, and garnish with parsley.

PORK CHOPS AND SAUERKRAUT
MAKES 8 SERVINGS   7.4 GRAMS PER SERVING

16 center-cut pork chops, ½-inch thick
2 tablespoons bacon drippings
Salt and freshly ground pepper
2 tablespoons prepared hot mustard (Dijon or Düsseldorf)
2 pounds sauerkraut, drained
1 cup diced peeled tart green apples
1 teaspoon caraway seeds
8 slices of crisp bacon, diced

Brown well-trimmed chops on both sides in bacon drippings. Sprinkle with salt and pepper and rub mustard into both sides of chops. Combine sauerkraut, apples, and caraway seeds in large casserole and arrange chops, slightly overlapping, on top.

Preheat oven to 350° F. Tightly cover and bake ½ hour. Uncover and bake ½ hour longer. Transfer chops and sauerkraut to deep, heated platter and sprinkle with crisp bacon.

STUFFED PORK CHOPS
MAKES 8 SERVINGS   6.4 GRAMS PER SERVING

8 double loin pork chops, with pockets
Salt and freshly ground pepper
½ cup minced onions
¼ cup minced celery
¼ teaspoon minced garlic
2 tablespoons butter or margarine
1½ cups soft rye bread cubes
¼ cup chopped fresh parsley
1 egg, lightly beaten
1½ cups strong bouillon
1 tablespoon vegetable oil
1 tablespoon soy sauce
¼ teaspoon sweet basil
1 teaspoon cornstarch
Chopped fresh parsley

Sprinkle well-trimmed chops with salt and pepper. Sauté onions, celery, and garlic in butter until tender. Add bread cubes, parsley, salt, and pepper. Moisten with egg and 2 tablespoons of bouillon. Toss. Stuff chops with bread mixture, close, and secure with toothpicks or skewers. Sear chops on both sides in large Dutch oven brushed with oil.

Preheat oven to 350° F. Cover and bake 30 minutes. Drain pan drippings. Combine remaining consommé, soy sauce, and sweet basil, and pour over chops. Uncover and continue to bake 30 minutes or until chops are tender when tested with a fork. Remove chops to heated platter. Make a smooth paste of cornstarch and water. Stir into sauce, scrape sides and bottom of pan, simmer until sauce thickens. Pour sauce over chops and garnish with parsley.

CROWN ROAST OF PORK WITH APPLE STUFFING
MAKES 8 SERVINGS   7.3 GRAMS PER SERVING

1 16-chop crown roast of pork	1 teaspoon grated lemon rind
Salt and freshly ground pepper	⅛ teaspoon cinnamon
1 tablespoon chopped onions	Freshly grated nutmeg
½ cup chopped celery	½ teaspoon salt
1 tablespoon vegetable oil	1½ tablespoons Calvados or
1 cup toasted protein bread cubes	applejack
	Paper frills
2 cups diced peeled tart apples	Watercress
	Spiced love apples

Have your butcher prepare a crown roast of pork and remove excess fat. Salt and pepper all surfaces and cover the tips of chops with aluminum foil to prevent charring. Insert meat thermometer away from bones.

Preheat oven to 450° F.

Place roast in roasting pan in oven and immediately reduce heat to 350° F. Bake for 2½ hours and pour off pan drippings. In a skillet, sauté onions and celery in oil until tender. Add bread cubes, apples, lemon rind, cinnamon, nutmeg, and salt. Moisten with brandy and toss lightly to mix. Spoon stuffing into the center of the crown, cover stuffing with aluminum foil and continue to bake 1 hour and 15 minutes or until meat thermometer reads 185° F. Remove foil from over stuffing and from the tips of chops, replacing foil with paper frills. Carefully transfer roast to heated platter and garnish with watercress and spiced love apples.

HERBED PORK ROAST
MAKES 8 SERVINGS   2.3 GRAMS PER SERVING

1 6- to 7-pound loin pork roast
Olive or vegetable oil
½ teaspoon thyme
½ teaspoon oregano
2 teaspoons salt
1 teaspoon freshly ground
  pepper
½ cup thinly sliced onions
½ cup sliced peeled carrots
½ cup sliced celery
½ cup chopped onions

½ teaspoon minced garlic
2 whole cloves
1 bay leaf
Freshly grated nutmeg
1¼ cups dry white wine
1¼ cups beef bouillon
1 tablespoon fresh lemon
  juice
2 tablespoons flour
2 tablespoons butter or
  margarine

Rub meat with oil and press mixture of thyme, oregano, salt, and pepper into meat. Place sliced onions on top of roast, cover closely with plastic wrap, and refrigerate overnight. Arrange carrots, celery, chopped onions, garlic, cloves, and bay leaf in bottom of roasting pan and sprinkle generously with nutmeg. Pour in ½ cup each of wine and bouillon. Place roast, rib side down, on top of vegetables and spread sliced onions on top. Insert meat thermometer into meat away from bones.

Preheat oven to 475° F. and bake 20 minutes. Reduce heat to 350° F. and bake 3½ hours or until meat thermometer reads 185° F. Baste occasionally without washing away sliced onions. Transfer roast and sliced onions to heated platter and sprinkle with lemon juice.

Strain, discarding vegetables, and skim off fat from cooking liquid. Stir in remaining wine and bouillon, scrape sides and bottom of pan, bring to a rapid boil, and reduce to 1 cup. Combine flour and butter and stir into reduced liquid. Simmer for 5 minutes and serve gravy separately.

BARBECUED SPARERIBS
MAKES 8 SERVINGS   4.5 GRAMS PER SERVING

3 racks of pork spareribs (about 9 pounds)	3 tablespoons dry sherry
	¾ teaspoon ground ginger
¼ cup tomato sauce	1½ tablespoons honey
3 tablespoons soy sauce	1¼ teaspoons salt
1 teaspoon minced garlic	1 teaspoon paprika

Preheat oven to 300° F. Cut spareribs into 4-inch pieces, placing them on a rack in baking pan, and bake 45 minutes. Drain pan drippings and place spareribs directly in baking pan. Combine remaining ingredients in saucepan, bring to a boil, and simmer 5 minutes. Brush spareribs with barbecue sauce and bake 30 minutes longer. Brush with additional sauce occasionally to prevent charring. Turn spareribs and brush with remaining sauce and bake 30 minutes longer, basting frequently with sauce in pan. Transfer spareribs to serving platter and spoon sauce over ribs.

POULTRY

SAMPLE POULTRY MENUS

Eggs in aspic*
*Chicken with almonds**
Buttered spinach
Tossed green salad
Petit pot de crème*

Cream of watercress soup*
*Chicken Italienne**
Fresh green beans
Sliced mushroom salad*
Zabaglione*

Jellied chicken consommé with
   lemon wedge
*Chicken Divan**
Broiled tomatoes*
Endive salad
Coeur à la crème*

Consommé with quenelles*
*Chicken Gismonda**
Tossed green salad
Peaches royale*

Borscht*
*Chicken Kiev**
Buttered spinach
Caesar salad*
Persian melon with lemon
   wedge

Pâté de foie gras
*Chicken with lemon cream
   sauce**
Green beans and mushrooms*
Tossed green salad
Coffee Bavarian cream*

Caviar Madrilène*
*Chicken paprika**
Spinach soufflé*
Tossed green salad
Strawberries Romanoff*

Eggs in aspic*
Chicken tarragon
Eggplant Parmigiana*
Boston lettuce salad
Fresh fruit and cheese*

Onion soup*
Coq au vin
Braised celery*
Wilted spinach salad*
Honeydew melon with lemon
  wedge

Jellied Madrilène with lemon
  wedge
Duck à l'orange
Fresh asparagus
Cucumber and onion salad*
Frozen Grand Marnier mousse*

Petite marmite*
Turkey Florentine
Broiled tomatoes*
Tossed green salad
Coupe de luxe*

CHICKEN WITH ALMONDS

MAKES 8 SERVINGS   6.4 GRAMS PER SERVING

2 3-pound chickens, each cut into 8 pieces	¼ cup blanched crushed almonds
¼ cup butter or margarine	¾ cup blanched almond slivers
¼ teaspoon chopped garlic	1 teaspoon dried tarragon
2 tablespoons chopped onions	Salt and freshly ground pepper
2 tablespoons flour	¾ cup sour cream
1½ cups chicken broth	2 tablespoons freshly grated Parmesan cheese
2 tablespoons sherry	
1 tablespoon tomato paste	

Brown chicken in butter on all sides in Dutch oven. Set aside. Sauté garlic and onions in Dutch oven until tender. Sprinkle with flour and stir until smooth. Stir in chicken broth, sherry, and tomato paste and bring to a boil. Add chicken, crushed almonds, ¼ cup of almond slivers, tarragon, salt, and pepper. Cover and simmer very slowly for 45 minutes or until chicken is tender. Transfer chicken to shallow ovenproof serving platter. Stir sour cream into sauce and pour over chicken. Sprinkle with remaining almond slivers and cheese. Brown under broiler and serve piping hot.

CHICKEN ITALIENNE
MAKES 8 SERVINGS   3.5 GRAMS PER SERVING

4 chicken breasts, skinned,
   boned, and halved
¼ cup olive or vegetable oil
Salt and freshly ground pepper
8 slices prosciutto ham
8 slices Mozzarella cheese
1 cup diced onions

¼ teaspoon minced garlic
2 tablespoons butter or
   margarine
1 cup peeled seeded tomatoes,
   quartered
½ teaspoon dried thyme
½ teaspoon dried oregano

Brown chicken on both sides in olive oil and sprinkle with salt and pepper. Arrange browned pieces in single layer in buttered baking dish. On each chicken breast, place a slice of prosciutto topped with cheese. Sauté onions and garlic in butter until tender. Add tomatoes, spices, salt, and pepper and simmer for 15 minutes. Strain liquid from sauce into a saucepan, bring to a rapid boil, and reduce by half. Add tomatoes and stir. Pour tomato sauce over chicken.

Preheat oven to 350° F. and bake 20 minutes or until chicken is tender.

CHICKEN DIVAN
MAKES 8 SERVINGS   7.1 GRAMS PER SERVING

3 tablespoons softened butter
   or margarine
3 tablespoons flour
2 cups chicken broth
¼ cup dry sherry
1 teaspoon Worcestershire
   sauce
¾ cup freshly grated
   Parmesan cheese

¼ teaspoon freshly grated
   nutmeg
Salt and freshly ground white
   pepper
¾ cup Hollandaise sauce
   (see *Sauces*)
1½ pounds cooked fresh
   broccoli
½ cup heavy cream, whipped
3 pounds cooked sliced white
   chicken (or turkey) meat

Blend butter and flour and stir into broth. Simmer 10 minutes, stirring occasionally until thickened. Remove from heat. Stir in sherry, Worcestershire sauce, ½ cup Parmesan cheese, nutmeg, salt, and pepper and simmer until cheese melts. Stir in Hollandaise.

Pour half of sauce over broccoli on a shallow ovenproof serving platter. Place chicken on top. Fold whipped cream into remaining sauce and pour over chicken. Sprinkle with remaining cheese.

Preheat oven to 400° F. and bake divan about 12 minutes or until nicely browned and sauce bubbles.

CHICKEN GISMONDA

MAKES 8 SERVINGS   8.3 GRAMS PER SERVING

4 chicken breasts, skinned, boned and halved	4 tablespoons butter or margarine
1 egg, lightly beaten	⅛ teaspoon freshly grated nutmeg
1 tablespoon water	
¼ cup freshly grated Parmesan cheese	1 teaspoon fresh lemon juice
½ cup dry bread crumbs	1 pound fresh mushrooms, sliced
1 teaspoon salt	2 tablespoons sherry
2 cups chopped cooked spinach	Oil for deep frying
	Chopped fresh parsley

Pound chicken between few layers of waxed paper with wooden mallet or rolling pin until ⅛ inch thick. Combine egg and water. Combine Parmesan cheese, bread crumbs, and salt. Dip chicken into egg mixture and then into cheese mixture. Refrigerate for 1 hour or longer. Thoroughly drain cooked spinach and add 2 tablespoons of butter, nutmeg, and lemon juice. Cover and keep hot.

Sauté the mushrooms in 2 tablespoons of butter until tender. Stir in sherry, cover, and keep hot. Heat 1 inch of oil to 375° F. or until a cube of bread dropped into it browns easily. Slowly immerse chicken in hot oil and fry for 5 minutes or until chicken is nicely browned. Drain thoroughly.

Arrange eight individual servings of hot spinach on large heated platter or individual dinner plates and place piece of chicken on each. Overlap mushroom slices on top of chicken and spoon mushroom pan liquid over each serving. Sprinkle with chopped parsley and serve piping hot.

CHICKEN KIEV

MAKES 8 SERVINGS   5.0 GRAMS PER SERVING

4 chicken breasts, skinned, boned, and halved
Salt and freshly ground white pepper
8 large fresh mushrooms, minced
1 tablespoon butter or margarine
½ pound sweet butter, softened
½ teaspoon minced garlic
2 tablespoons minced fresh parsley
2 eggs, lightly beaten
1 tablespoon vodka or water
½ cup very fine bread crumbs
¼ pound butter or margarine

Pound chicken between few layers of waxed paper with wooden mallet or rolling pin until as thin as possible without breaking flesh. Carefully remove paper and sprinkle chicken lightly with salt and pepper. Sauté mushrooms in butter for 3 minutes or until tender. Drain.

Cream sweet butter, garlic, parsley, and mushrooms together. Chill slightly and shape into 8 oval rolls, 2 by ¾ inches in diameter. Set aside in iced water to harden. Dry butter rolls thoroughly and wrap flattened chicken breasts around each roll, envelope style, so butter is completely encased. Chicken will adhere to itself without skewers or string. Combine eggs and vodka. Dip rolled chicken into this mixture, then roll in bread crumbs. Repeat and refrigerate for 1 hour or longer.

Preheat oven to 400° F. Sauté chicken in butter over medium heat until outside is golden brown. Drain on paper towels, place on baking sheet and bake 10 minutes. Serve immediately.

CHICKEN WITH LEMON CREAM SAUCE
MAKES 8 SERVINGS 2.2 GRAMS PER SERVING

2 3-pound chickens, each cut into 8 pieces
3 tablespoons butter or margarine
6 tablespoons olive or vegetable oil
1½ tablespoons sherry
1½ tablespoons dry white wine or vermouth
1 tablespoon grated lemon rind
1 tablespoon grated orange rind
1 tablespoon fresh lemon juice
Salt and freshly ground white pepper
1¼ cups light cream
Freshly grated Parmesan cheese
Thin lemon slices
Chopped fresh parsley

Brown chicken in butter and oil. Cover, lower heat, and simmer slowly for 40 minutes or until chicken is tender. Drain well and arrange chicken on an ovenproof serving platter and keep warm. Discard cooking oil. Stir sherry, wine, lemon rind, orange rind, lemon juice, salt, and pepper into same skillet. Slowly stir in cream, cover, and simmer 2 minutes. Pour sauce over chicken and sprinkle with Parmesan cheese. Brown slightly under preheated broiler and garnish with lemon slices sprinkled with chopped parsley.

CHICKEN PAPRIKA
MAKES 8 SERVINGS 2.0 GRAMS PER SERVING

½ cup thinly sliced red onions
¼ teaspoon minced garlic
3 tablespoons butter or margarine
1 tablespoon Hungarian paprika
1 teaspoon fresh lemon juice or tarragon vinegar
2 3-pound chickens, each cut into 8 pieces
¾ cup chicken broth
¼ cup dry sherry
Salt and freshly ground pepper
½ cup sour cream
Chopped fresh parsley

Sauté onions and garlic in butter until tender in heavy casserole. Stir in paprika and lemon juice. Add chicken and sauté lightly for 5 minutes, turning once to coat chicken evenly. Add chicken broth and sherry and sprinkle with salt and pepper. Cover and simmer 45 minutes or until chicken is tender. Remove chicken to heated platter. Stir in sour cream, scrape sides and bottom of casserole, and heat without boiling. Pour sauce over chicken and sprinkle with parsley.

CHICKEN TARRAGON
MAKES 8 SERVINGS   1.1 GRAMS PER SERVING

4 1½-pound chickens, halved with backbones removed	2 teaspoons crushed dried tarragon
1 garlic clove, halved	Salt and freshly ground pepper
1½ cups dry vermouth	¼ pound butter or margarine
3 tablespoons fresh lime juice	

Rub chickens with freshly cut garlic and place, skin side down, in shallow broiling pan. Pour 1 cup of vermouth into pan. Sprinkle chicken with half of lime juice, tarragon, salt, and pepper and dot liberally with butter. Broil chicken slowly about 4 inches from heat. Baste with pan drippings every 10 minutes, but do not wash away tarragon.

When chicken starts to brown, turn and sprinkle skin side with remaining lime juice, tarragon, salt, and pepper and dot liberally with butter. Baste every 10 minutes as before and turn chicken each time it starts to brown to prevent overbrowning. Chicken should be evenly browned and tender in 30 to 40 minutes. Remove to heated platter. Add remaining ½ cup of vermouth to broiling pan, scrape sides and bottom of pan, and heat. Pour hot sauce over chicken and serve.

COQ AU VIN
MAKES 8 SERVINGS   6.0 GRAMS PER SERVING

4 slices lean bacon, diced
4 tablespoons butter or
   margarine
2 3-pound chickens, each cut
   into 8 pieces
¼ cup warm cognac or brandy
2 tablespoons flour
¼ teaspoon thyme

1 tablespoon chopped fresh
   parsley
Freshly grated nutmeg
Salt and freshly ground pepper
1 bay leaf
16 small pearl onions, peeled
¾ pound whole mushrooms
¼ teaspoon minced garlic
3 cups Burgundy wine

Preheat oven to 300° F.

Sauté bacon in large heavy casserole until crisp and set aside. Add butter to casserole and brown chicken evenly on all sides. Drain. Pour warm cognac over chicken and ignite. When flame goes out, sprinkle in bacon, flour, thyme, parsley, nutmeg, salt, and pepper. Add remaining ingredients and stir. Cover and simmer 5 minutes. Transfer to preheated oven and bake 2½ hours or until chicken is tender. Discard bay leaf. Serve piping hot.

DUCK À L'ORANGE
MAKES 8 SERVINGS   8.3 GRAMS PER SERVING

2 4- to 5-pound ducklings
2 oranges
1 lemon
¼ cup brandy
2 cups dry red wine
½ cup chopped celery stalks
   with leaves
½ cup chopped peeled carrots
½ cup chopped onions

2 tablespoons chopped fresh
   parsley
3 tablespoons strong beef
   bouillon
1 tablespoon arrowroot
   (optional)
¼ cup Grand Marnier
2 cans mandarin orange
   sections (sugar free), drained

Trim ducklings of excess fat at base of tail and inside neck and body cavities. Prick skin with sharp fork or knife to allow fat to drain during roasting. Thinly peel rind from oranges and lemon and cut into julienne strips. Cover strips with water and boil 3 minutes. Drain and set aside. Squeeze juice from fruit, combine with brandy, and rub inside and outside of ducks with the mixture. Reserve remaining liquid.

Preheat oven to 400° F. Place ducklings in shallow roasting pan and roast 1 hour. Pour off all but 2 tablespoons of fat. Combine red wine, chopped vegetables, parsley, bouillon, and fruit juice–brandy mixture and pour around ducks. Continue to roast 40 minutes longer (basting frequently) or until juices run clear when thigh joint is pricked. Remove ducklings to a heated platter and cut each into quarters.

Strain pan drippings and discard vegetables. Pour juice back into roasting pan, bring to a boil, scrape sides and bottom of pan, and reduce to 1½ cups. Thicken with arrowroot, if necessary. Add Grand Marnier, orange and lemon slivers, and orange sections. Simmer until heated through and pour sauce over ducks.

TURKEY FLORENTINE
MAKES 8 SERVINGS   4.2 GRAMS PER SERVING

1¼ cups Allemande sauce
   (see *Sauces*)
4 cups cooked chopped
   spinach

3 pounds cooked white turkey
   (or chicken) meat, thinly
   sliced
6 tablespoons freshly grated
   Parmesan cheese

Stir ½ cup of sauce into well drained spinach and heat thoroughly without boiling. Spoon spinach onto ovenproof serving platter and place sliced turkey on top. Stir 4 tablespoons of Parmesan cheese into remaining sauce and pour over turkey slices. Dot with butter and sprinkle with remaining cheese.

Preheat broiler. Brown lightly 5 inches from heat until heated through and serve piping hot.

SEAFOOD

SAMPLE SEAFOOD MENUS

*Bouillabaisse Americana**
Crisp fresh spinach salad
Persian melon with lemon
   wedge

Avgolemono soup*
*Brook trout Meunière**
Spinach soufflé*
Sliced mushroom salad*
Fresh fruit and cheese*

Eggs in aspic*
*Coquilles Saint-Jacques**
Fresh asparagus
Tossed green salad
Petit pot de crème*

Cold curried avocado soup*
*Deviled crab**
Broiled tomatoes*
Cole slaw*
Coupe de luxe*

Lobster cocktail*
*Soft-shelled crabs amandine**
Spinach soufflé*
Sliced mushroom salad*
Fresh fruit compote

Onion soup*
*Frogs' legs Provençale**
Broiled tomatoes*
Crisp fresh spinach salad
Fresh fruit and cheese*

Oysters Rockefeller*
*Lobster Newburg**
Fresh asparagus
Tossed green salad
Fresh fruit and cheese*

Cream of watercress soup*
*Cold stuffed lobster**
Fresh strawberries and mandarin
   orange sections

87

Crab cocktail*
*Moules marinière**
Crisp fresh spinach salad
Casaba melon

Cherrystone clams on the half
shell with lemon wedge
*Baked stuffed red snapper**
Broccoli Allemande*
Sliced mushroom salad*
Coupe de luxe*

Billi Bi*
*Salmon mousse**
Endive and watercress salad
Dessert cheeses*

Seafood in shells*
*Broiled salmon steak tarragon**
Green beans with mushrooms*
Tossed green salad
Blancmange with red
raspberries*

Prosciutto and melon*
*Scampi**
Buttered spinach
Tossed green salad
Zabaglione*

Shrimp cocktail with lemon
wedge
*Broiled scrod with pecan sauce**
Fresh asparagus
Beet and onion salad*
Peaches royale*

Cold tomato soup*
*Sautéed shad roe**
Green beans with dill
Tossed green salad
Honeydew melon with lime
wedge

Billi Bi*
*Shrimp de Jonghe**
Broiled tomatoes*
Boston lettuce salad
Dessert cheeses*

Lobster bisque*
*Fillet of sole with white wine
sauce**
Fresh asparagus
Mushrooms stuffed with
anchovies*
Tossed green salad
Sliced apples and mandarin
orange sections

BOUILLABAISSE AMERICANA

MAKES 8 SERVINGS 7.2 GRAMS PER SERVING

½ cup chopped onions
¼ cup chopped celery
¼ cup chopped leeks
½ teaspoon minced garlic
½ teaspoon thyme
½ bay leaf
2 tablespoons olive or vegetable oil
2 tomatoes, peeled, seeded and chopped
1 cup clam juice
1 cup dry white wine
2 tablespoons chopped fresh parsley
¼ teaspoon crushed or ⅛ teaspoon ground fennel seeds

2 inch piece of lemon rind
⅛ teaspoon saffron
Salt and freshly ground pepper
8 oysters, scrubbed
16 mussels, scrubbed and debearded
16 small clams, scrubbed
1 cup fresh crab meat
1 cup fresh lobster meat
16 raw shrimp, shelled and deveined
1 pound red snapper, cod, or haddock, cut into bite-size pieces
Chopped fresh parsley

Sauté onions, celery, leeks, garlic, thyme, and bay leaf in large kettle in oil for 5 minutes or until vegetables are tender and golden brown. Discard bay leaf. Add tomatoes, clam juice, wine, parsley, fennel seeds, lemon rind, saffron, salt, and pepper. Stir, scrape sides and bottom of kettle, and simmer 15 minutes. Bring soup to a rapid boil. Add seafood and bring to a rapid boil again. Boil 10 minutes or until fish is just tender when tested with a fork. Add additional salt and pepper, if needed. Serve piping hot garnished with chopped parsley.

BROOK TROUT MEUNIÈRE

MAKES 8 SERVINGS 3.9 GRAMS PER SERVING

8 brook trout, cleaned
Milk
½ cup flour
½ teaspoon salt
Freshly ground pepper

Peanut oil
½ cup Meunière butter (see *Sauces*)
Lemon wedges

Dip trout in milk and drain well. Lightly coat trout with flour seasoned with salt and pepper. Heat ¼ inch of peanut oil in heavy skillet and sauté fish about 5 minutes on each side or until golden brown. Remove to a heated platter. Drain oil from skillet and wipe with paper towel. Prepare Meunière butter in skillet and pour over trout. Serve piping hot garnished with lemon wedges.

COQUILLES SAINT-JACQUES
MAKES 8 SERVINGS   5.7 GRAMS PER SERVING

2 cups dry white wine	1½ tablespoons minced
1 tablespoon chopped fresh	scallions
parsley	4 tablespoons butter or
⅛ teaspoon thyme	margarine
⅛ teaspoon marjoram	1½ tablespoons flour
Salt	2 egg yolks, lightly beaten
6 peppercorns	2 tablespoons heavy cream
2 pounds fresh scallops	3 tablespoons freshly grated
1 cup chopped fresh	Parmesan cheese
mushrooms	Paprika

Combine wine, parsley, thyme, marjoram, salt, and peppercorns and simmer 5 minutes. Add scallops, cover, and simmer 2 minutes or until scallops become very white. Drain and cut scallops in two or four pieces depending on their size. Strain and reserve 1½ cups of broth. Sauté mushrooms and scallions in 2 tablespoons of butter until tender. Sprinkle with flour and stir until smooth. Combine broth with egg yolks and cream. Slowly stir mixture into skillet and add scallops. Stir over low heat for 1 minute and cool. Spoon equal portions of scallop mixture into eight well-buttered deep scallop shells or ramekins. Dot with butter and sprinkle with Parmesan cheese and paprika.

Preheat oven to 400° F. Bake coquilles 5 to 10 minutes or until bubbling and golden brown.

DEVILED CRAB
MAKES 8 SERVINGS   2.5 GRAMS PER SERVING

16 hard-shelled crabs
2 tablespoons minced onions
2 tablespoons minced green peppers
4 tablespoons butter or margarine
1 tablespoon chopped chives
1 tablespoon prepared hot mustard (Dijon or Düsseldorf)
1 teaspoon Worcestershire sauce
2 drops Tabasco
1/4 teaspoon freshly grated pepper
Salt and cayenne pepper
2 tablespoons cream
2 tablespoons sherry or rum
2 tablespoons fine bread crumbs
2 tablespoons freshly grated Parmesan cheese
Fresh parsley clusters
Lemon wedges

Cook hard-shelled crabs in boiling salted water for 15 minutes or until shells turn red. Flake meat, carefully removing all shells and tendons, and place in large mixing bowl. Scrub and reserve eight of handsomest shells. Sauté onions and peppers in 2 tablespoons of butter until tender and add to crab meat. Add chives, mustard, Worcestershire sauce, Tabasco, pepper, salt, and cayenne pepper. Moisten with cream and sherry and mix thoroughly. Spoon equal portions of crab mixture into individual buttered crab shells or ramekins. Sprinkle each serving with combination of bread crumbs and cheese and dot liberally with butter.

Preheat oven to 400° F. Bake 20 minutes or until well browned. Garnish with clusters of parsley and lemon wedges.

SOFT-SHELLED CRABS AMANDINE
MAKES 8 SERVINGS 7.1 GRAMS PER SERVING

16 soft-shelled crabs, prepared for sautéeing
1 quart milk
4 egg yolks, well beaten
2 tablespoons chopped fresh parsley
2 tablespoons chopped chives
2 tablespoons chopped celery leaves
2 tablespoons chopped onions
2 tablespoons chopped leeks
¼ teaspoon crushed garlic
¼ teaspoon crushed dried thyme
¼ teaspoon crushed dried tarragon
⅛ teaspoon freshly grated nutmeg
Salt and freshly ground white pepper
½ cup seasoned flour
½ pound butter or margarine
1 cup almond butter (see *Sauces*)
Chopped chives
Lemon wedges

Carefully wash soft-shelled crabs and place in large bowl or casserole. Combine all ingredients (except flour, butter, almond butter, chives, and lemon wedges) and pour over crabs. Cover bowl and marinate 30 minutes. Crabs will absorb some milk and flavors. Carefully remove crabs from milk mixture and dip in flour seasoned with salt and pepper.

Sauté crabs in butter for 5 minutes on each side or until golden brown. Carefully remove crabs to heated platter. Prepare almond butter sauce with butter remaining in skillet. Spoon almonds (not butter) over crabs and sprinkle with chopped chives. Garnish with lemon wedges.

FROGS' LEGS PROVENÇALE
MAKES 8 SERVINGS   3.0 GRAMS PER SERVING

¼ cup fresh lemon juice
2 cups water
6 dozen medium-sized frogs' legs
¼ cup flour
Salt and freshly ground white pepper

Peanut oil
½ teaspoon minced garlic
¼ pound butter or margarine
2 tablespoons fresh lemon juice or white wine vinegar
3 tablespoons chopped fresh parsley

Combine lemon juice and water in large bowl. Immerse frogs' legs and wash them well. Drain and dry thoroughly. Dust frogs' legs with flour seasoned with salt and pepper.

Sauté frogs' legs in 1 inch of hot peanut oil for 6 to 8 minutes or until golden brown on both sides. Drain and discard oil. Pile frogs' legs in pyramid on heated platter. Sauté garlic in butter in same skillet until golden brown. Stir in lemon juice or vinegar and pour sauce over frogs' legs. Sprinkle with parsley and serve piping hot.

LOBSTER NEWBURG
MAKES 8 SERVINGS   2.7 GRAMS PER SERVING

2 pounds cooked fresh lobster meat, diced
4 tablespoons butter or margarine
½ teaspoon paprika
½ cup dry sherry
1½ cups heavy cream

4 egg yolks, well beaten
¼ teaspoon dry mustard
Salt and freshly ground white pepper
Lobster coral, crumbled (if available)
Chopped fresh parsley

Sauté lobster meat in butter for 3 minutes. Sprinkle with paprika and stir in sherry. Cook until wine almost disappears. Combine cream, egg yolks, mustard, salt, and pepper in top of double boiler. Stir in lobster mixture and heat gently until sauce thickens slightly. Spoon into individual scallop shells or lobster shells. Sprinkle with lobster coral and chopped parsley and serve piping hot.

COLD STUFFED LOBSTER

MAKES 8 SERVINGS   2.1 GRAMS PER SERVING

8 1- to 1¼-pound cooked
   lobsters
2 tablespoons minced onions
6 tablespoons melted butter or
   margarine
½ cup mayonnaise or Miracle
   Whip
1 tablespoon prepared hot
   mustard (Dijon or Düsseldorf)

1 tablespoon fresh lemon juice
1 pound cooked crab meat,
   carefully shelled
⅛ teaspoon thyme
Freshly grated nutmeg
¼ teaspoon salt
Fresh parsley or watercress

Split each lobster in half and remove sand sac near top of head and intestines. Press coral, green liver, and roe through sieve and reserve. Sauté onions in 2 tablespoons of butter until tender. Combine coral mixture, onions, remaining melted butter, mayonnaise, mustard, lemon juice, crab meat, thyme, nutmeg, and salt. Mix thoroughly. Stuff each lobster body with crab meat mixture and garnish with parsley or watercress.

MOULES MARINIÈRE

MAKES 8 SERVINGS   5.0 GRAMS PER SERVING

4 quarts fresh mussels
1½ cups dry white wine
½ cup chopped onions
1 tablespoon chopped
   shallots
¼ cup parsley sprigs
¼ teaspoon thyme

1 small bay leaf
Freshly ground pepper
Cayenne pepper
¼ pound butter or margarine
Salt (if needed)
2 tablespoons chopped fresh
   parsley

Scrub mussels with stiff brush to remove all sand and beards. Refrigerate until ready to use. Boil wine, onions, shallots, parsley, thyme, bay leaf, pepper, and cayenne in large kettle for 5 minutes. Add mussels, cover, and bring to rapid boil again. Boil 5 to 10 minutes. Lift and stir mussels occasionally. Remove mussels from broth. Discard all unopened shells and top shell from each opened mussel. Arrange mussels in individual soup dishes. Strain broth through cloth-lined sieve into a saucepan. Heat and stir in butter. Add salt (if needed) and pour over mussels. Sprinkle with chopped parsley and serve piping hot.

BAKED STUFFED RED SNAPPER
MAKES 8 SERVINGS   6.8 GRAMS PER SERVING

1 4- to 5-pound red snapper	2 tablespoons fresh lemon
Fresh lime or lemon juice	juice
Salt and freshly ground pepper	¼ teaspoon thyme or basil
3 tablespoons minced onions	1 tablespoon minced fresh
2 tablespoons minced celery	parsley
4 tablespoons butter or	2 cups dry white wine
margarine	Lemon wedges
1 cup chopped cooked shrimp	Watercress
1 cup cooked rice	

Wipe red snapper with paper towels and sprinkle with lime juice and salt. Refrigerate for 2 or 3 hours. Sauté onions and celery in butter until tender. Stir in shrimp, rice, lemon juice, thyme, parsley, salt, and pepper. Place fish on top of well-buttered sheet of heavy duty aluminum foil which overlaps ends of shallow baking pan. Fill fish cavity with stuffing and close with skewers and string. Carefully cut 3 or 4 slits through skin to prevent fish from changing shape during cooking.

Preheat oven to 350° F. Pour wine around fish and bake 1 hour or until fish flakes easily when tested with a fork. Baste occasionally with pan juices. Lift fish from baking pan, using foil as a cradle, and slide it onto heated platter. Garnish with lemon wedges and watercress.

SALMON MOUSSE

MAKES 8 SERVINGS   2.4 GRAMS PER SERVING

1 envelope unflavored gelatin
1 tablespoon fresh lemon juice
1 tablespoon chopped onion
½ cup boiling water
2 cups canned salmon, drained
½ cup mayonnaise
¼ teaspoon Tabasco sauce
¼ teaspoon paprika
1 teaspoon dried dill
1 teaspoon salt
1 cup heavy cream
4 hard-cooked eggs, quartered
Watercress
2 cups horseradish mousseline
  sauce (see *Sauces*)

Combine gelatin, lemon juice, onion, and water in electric blender. Cover and blend at high speed for 40 seconds. Scrape sides of blender with rubber spatula. Add salmon, mayonnaise, Tabasco sauce, paprika, dill, and salt. Cover and blend at high speed. Remove cover while motor is on and slowly add cream. Re-cover and blend no more than 30 seconds.

Pour mousse into 4-cup oiled fish mold and chill until set.

To unmold, dip mold in warm water, wipe mold dry, and immediately invert on large serving platter. Garnish with hard-cooked eggs and watercress. Serve horseradish mousseline sauce separately.

BROILED SALMON STEAK TARRAGON

MAKES 8 SERVINGS   1.2 GRAMS PER SERVING

1 cup dry vermouth
8 fresh salmon steaks, 1 inch
  thick
¼ cup fresh lime juice
½ pound butter or margarine
1 teaspoon crushed dried
  tarragon
Salt and freshly ground pepper
Lime wedges
Watercress or fresh parsley

Pour vermouth around salmon steaks in shallow well-buttered baking pan. Sprinkle each steak with generous amount of lime juice, a pinch of tarragon, salt, and pepper. Dot with 4 tablespoons of butter.

Preheat broiler. Broil steaks 4 inches from heat for 10 minutes. After 5 minutes, baste carefully so as not to wash away tarragon. Turn steaks and season as before. Broil 5 minutes and baste carefully again to prevent browning. Serve garnished with lime wedges and watercress.

SCAMPI

MAKES 8 SERVINGS   2.1 GRAMS PER SERVING

1 teaspoon minced garlic	1/2 teaspoon basil
1/4 pound butter or margarine	1/2 teaspoon oregano
1/4 cup olive or vegetable oil	3/4 teaspoon salt
1 tablespoon fresh lemon juice	Freshly ground pepper
2 drops Tabasco	48 jumbo shrimp, shelled (tails
1 tablespoon chopped fresh	intact) and deveined
parsley	Lemon wedges

Sauté garlic in butter and oil for 2 minutes. Add lemon juice, Tabasco, parsley, basil, oregano, salt, and pepper and simmer for 2 minutes. Split shrimp halfway through inside seam and spread open like butterflies. Dip shrimp in butter mixture and place in a shallow baking pan, tails turning up.

Preheat oven to 450° F. Bake shrimp for 5 minutes. Pour remaining butter mixture over them and place under broiler for 5 minutes longer or until browned. Serve sizzling hot garnished with lemon wedges.

BROILED SCROD WITH PECAN SAUCE
MAKES 8 SERVINGS   3.7 GRAMS PER SERVING

4 pounds fillet of scrod, 1 to
   1 ½ inches thick
½ cup vegetable or olive oil
1 teaspoon Worcestershire
   sauce
Dash Tabasco
¼ teaspoon paprika
¼ cup freshly grated Parmesan
   cheese

¼ cup fresh bread crumbs
Salt and freshly ground white
   pepper
½ cup coarsely chopped pecans
¼ cup butter or margarine
2 tablespoons chopped chives
   or parsley
Lemon wedges

Specially order thick fillets of scrod with skin intact. Combine oil, Worcestershire sauce, Tabasco, and paprika in shallow bowl. Combine cheese, bread crumbs, salt, and pepper in a separate bowl. Dip fillets in oil mixture then in cheese mixture. Arrange fillets, skin side down, on a generously buttered ovenproof serving platter. Dot with butter and sprinkle with pecans.

Preheat oven to 450° F. Brown fillets quickly under hot broiler to seal in juices. Transfer platter to oven and bake 10 to 15 minutes or until fish turns white in center and flakes easily when tested with fork. Do not overcook. Sprinkle with chives and garnish with lemon wedges. When serving try not to include skin.

SAUTÉED SHAD ROE
MAKES 8 SERVINGS   3.0 GRAMS PER SERVING

½ pound melted butter or
   margarine
8 pairs shad roe
Salt and freshly ground pepper
1 tablespoon fresh lemon juice

1 teaspoon chopped chives
Chopped fresh parsley
Lemon wedges
8 strips of crisp bacon, halved

Heat butter in large skillet until it foams. Add shad roe pairs, cover, and simmer 5 to 7 minutes. Turn very carefully so as not to break membrane covering. Season roe lightly with salt and pepper. Cover and simmer 5 to 7 minutes longer, making certain butter does not brown. Carefully remove roe to heated platter. Add lemon juice and chives to butter in skillet and scrape sides and bottom of pan. Spoon some butter over roe and sprinkle with parsley. Garnish with lemon wedges and top with crisp bacon slices.

SHRIMP DE JONGHE

MAKES 8 SERVINGS   6.0 GRAMS PER SERVING

4 pounds cooked shrimp, shelled and deveined
½ pound softened sweet butter or margarine
¼ teaspoon crushed garlic
¼ teaspoon minced shallots
¼ teaspoon tarragon
¼ teaspoon marjoram
Dash freshly grated nutmeg
½ cup dry sherry

Salt and freshly ground white pepper
3 tablespoons fine bread crumbs
2 tablespoons chopped fresh parsley
3 tablespoons butter or margarine
Parsley clusters

Place shrimp in well-buttered individual ramekins or large scallop shells. Combine softened butter with garlic, shallots, tarragon, marjoram, nutmeg, sherry, salt, and pepper. Cream until smooth. Spoon equal portions of butter mixture over shrimp and sprinkle with bread crumbs and parsley. Dot liberally with butter.

Preheat oven to 400° F. Bake shrimp 10 to 15 minutes or until lightly browned and sauce bubbles. Serve garnished with clusters of parsley.

FILLET OF SOLE WITH WHITE WINE SAUCE

MAKES 8 SERVINGS   1.8 GRAMS PER SERVING

8 fillets of sole
½ pound cooked crab meat, shelled and chopped
½ pound cooked shrimp, shelled, deveined, and chopped
4 tablespoons melted butter or margarine
2 tablespoons chopped onions
1 cup dry white wine
1 cup water
2 tablespoons fresh lemon juice
Salt and freshly ground white pepper
1 teaspoon cornstarch
3 egg yolks
¾ cup heavy cream
Lemon wedges
Watercress or fresh parsley clusters

Halve fillets lengthwise and cover each piece with thin layer of crab meat and shrimp. Roll and secure with toothpick. Pour melted butter in shallow baking pan and arrange fillets side by side. Sprinkle with onions. Combine wine, water, and lemon juice and pour around fillets. Sprinkle lightly with salt and pepper.

Preheat oven to 375° F. Bake 12 minutes or until fish is white in center. Transfer fillets to heated platter. Bring cooking liquid to a rapid boil and reduce to ⅔ cup. Dissolve cornstarch in 2 tablespoons of reduced liquid and stir into pan. Beat egg yolks lightly with cream. Stir into reduced liquid and heat, without boiling, until thickened. Strain over fish. Serve garnished with lemon wedges and watercress or parsley clusters.

VARIETY MEATS

SAMPLE VARIETY MEAT MENUS

Mushrooms à la Grecque*
*Brains au beurre noir**
Broiled tomatoes*
Crisp fresh spinach salad
Fresh fruit and cheese*

Avgolemono soup*
*Kidneys sauté à la moutarde**
Fresh asparagus
Tossed green salad
Coupe de luxe*

Seafood in shells*
*Broiled liver à la Béarnaise**
Green beans and mushrooms*
Cole slaw*
Dessert cheeses*

Philadelphia snapper soup*
*Braised sweetbreads**
Asparagus with Hollandaise*
Tossed green salad
Coupe de luxe*

Oysters casino*
*Braised tongue Tulare**
Buttered spinach
Stuffed mushrooms Parmigiana*
Cucumber and onion salad*
Cantaloupe with Cheddar cheese

Petite marmite*
*Tripe à la mode de Caen**
Fresh broccoli
Céleri rémoulade*
Fresh fruit and cheese*

BRAINS AU BEURRE NOIR

MAKES 8 SERVINGS   2.5 GRAMS PER SERVING

4 pairs veal brains
1 cup beef bouillon
¼ cup sliced onions
¼ cup sliced peeled carrots
¼ teaspoon thyme
1 bay leaf
1 teaspoon salt

5 peppercorns
4 tablespoons butter or margarine
2 tablespoons vegetable oil
¾ cup beurre noir (see *Sauces*)
2 tablespoons drained capers
Fresh parsley

Wash brains under running water and then soak in iced water to cover for 15 minutes. Combine bouillon, onions, carrots, thyme, bay leaf, salt, and peppercorns and boil 5 minutes. Add brains and boiling water to cover them by 2 inches. Reduce heat, cover, and simmer 20 minutes. Drain and plunge into iced water. When chilled and firm, trim away white opaque bits of fat. Cut into ½ -inch slices.

Sauté in butter and oil for 3 to 4 minutes on each side or until golden brown. Drain. Arrange browned slices on heated platter, sprinkle with capers, and pour beurre noir over them. Sprinkle with parsley and serve.

KIDNEYS SAUTÉ À LA MOUTARDE

MAKES 8 SERVINGS   5.1 GRAMS PER SERVING

6 veal kidneys
Salt and freshly ground pepper
3 tablespoons vegetable oil
5 tablespoons butter or margarine
2 tablespoons minced shallots
½ pound sliced mushrooms
½ cup dry white wine

2 cups brown sauce (see *Sauces*)
2 tablespoons prepared hot mustard (Dijon or Düsseldorf
3 tablespoons minced fresh parsley

Split and trim away tough center core of each kidney. Cut crosswise into thin slices and sprinkle with salt and pepper. Heat oil in heavy skillet, stir in kidneys, and sauté 3 minutes until browned but still rare. Pour into colander to drain. Wipe skillet with a paper towel. Add 2 tablespoons of butter, shallots, and mushrooms and sauté 1 minute over high heat, stirring constantly. Set aside.

Stir in wine, scraping sides and bottom of skillet, and cook until wine almost disappears.

Stir in brown sauce, kidneys, shallots, and mushrooms and bring to a boil. Stir in remaining 3 tablespoons of butter mixed with mustard. Add salt and pepper, if needed. Transfer kidneys to a deep, heated serving platter and sprinkle with parsley.

BROILED LIVER À LA BÉARNAISE
MAKES 8 SERVINGS   7.8 GRAMS PER SERVING

2 pounds calves' liver, ⅓-inch thick
¾ cup maître d'hôtel butter (see *Sauces*)
4 medium tomatoes, peeled and halved

½ pound watercress
Paprika
1 cup Béarnaise sauce (see *Sauces*)

Dip each slice of liver in melted butter sauce and set aside. Sauté tomato halves in remaining butter until barely tender but still firm.

Preheat broiler and broiler rack. Broil liver slices on preheated broiler rack 3 inches from heat for 1 minute. Turn and broil exactly 1 minute longer. Transfer liver to heated platter. Garnish each serving with tomato half and a generous amount of watercress dipped in paprika. Serve Béarnaise sauce separately.

BRAISED SWEETBREADS
MAKES 8 SERVINGS   2.0 GRAMS PER SERVING

4 pairs sweetbreads	3 tablespoons butter or
1 teaspoon lemon juice per	margarine
quart of water	1 tablespoon flour
½ cup sliced onions	Salt and freshly ground pepper
½ cup sliced peeled carrots	¾ cup dry white wine
¼ teaspoon thyme	1 cup chicken broth
1 tablespoon minced parsley	2 tablespoons dry sherry
1 bay leaf	Chopped fresh parsley
	Paprika

Wash sweetbreads under running water and soak in iced water to cover for 1 hour, changing water once. Drain sweetbreads and cover with fresh cold water (add 1 teaspoon of lemon juice per quart). Slowly bring to boil, lower heat, and simmer 5 minutes. Drain and plunge sweetbreads into iced water. When chilled and firm, trim away connecting tubes and tougher membranes, being careful not to break tissue.

Preheat oven to 350° F. Sauté onions, carrots, thyme, parsley, and bay leaf in butter for 5 minutes in large casserole. Sprinkle with flour, salt, and pepper. Stir in wine, bring to a rapid boil and reduce liquid to ½ cup. Add chicken broth and sweetbreads. Cover, place in bottom third of oven, and bake 25 minutes. Uncover casserole and bake 10 minutes longer or until sweetbreads break apart slightly when touched with a fork. Transfer sweetbreads to heated platter. Stir sherry into casserole and strain liquid over sweetbreads. Sprinkle with chopped parsley and paprika.

BRAISED TONGUE TULARE
MAKES 8 SERVINGS   7.2 GRAMS PER SERVING

2 pound fresh beef tongue
1 teaspoon salt per quart of
   water
6 sprigs fresh parsley
6 green celery tops
¼ teaspoon basil
¼ teaspoon marjoram
½ teaspoon thyme
1 large bay leaf
2 whole peppercorns
¼ cup flour

¼ cup butter or margarine
1 cup chopped peeled carrots
1 cup chopped celery
½ cup chopped onions
½ pound fresh mushrooms,
   sliced
1 cup dry white wine
1 cup tongue stock
1 tablespoon dried tarragon
1¼ cups Epicurean sauce (see
   Sauces)

Place tongue in large kettle and cover with salted water. Add parsley, celery tops, basil, marjoram, thyme, bay leaf, and peppercorns. Cover tightly and simmer 3 hours or until tender when tested with a fork. Let tongue cool in liquid. Strain and reserve stock. Skin and trim tongue. Rub with flour and brown in butter. Place in a casserole. Sauté chopped vegetables and sliced mushrooms until tender and add along with wine, stock, tarragon, and salt, if needed.

Preheat oven to 350° F. Bake 30 minutes or until top is browned and sauce thickens slightly. Transfer tongue to heated platter. Pour sauce over tongue and serve Epicurean sauce separately.

TRIPE À LA MODE DE CAEN

MAKES 8 SERVINGS   2.6 GRAMS PER SERVING

2 pound fresh honeycomb tripe
¼ pound fat salt pork
1 cup sliced onions
1 cup sliced peeled carrots
½ cup chopped celery
1 cup chopped green pepper
½ cup chopped leeks
1 cup chopped tomatoes, peeled and seeded
¼ teaspoon minced garlic
3 calves' feet, quartered
1 tablespoon chopped fresh parsley
¼ teaspoon thyme
¼ teaspoon marjoram
⅛ teaspoon mace
2 whole cloves
1 large bay leaf
1 teaspoon salt
8 bruised peppercorns
1 cup strong beef bouillon
1 cup dry white wine
¼ cup minced shallots
1 tablespoon butter or margarine
½ cup Calvados or applejack
Salt and freshly ground pepper
Fresh parsley

Preheat oven to 250° F.

Wash tripe thoroughly under cold, running water and cut into thin ½-by-2-inch strips. Line large earthenware casserole or Dutch oven with salt pork and vegetables. Add tripe and calves' feet and sprinkle with spices. Pour in bouillon and wine. Cover casserole with large sheet of aluminum foil then place lid on top to seal casserole completely. Bake overnight for 12 hours without removing cover.

Transfer tripe to deep heated platter or individual ramekins. Add meat from calves' feet and keep warm. Skim off fat and strain sauce through a cloth-lined sieve, discarding vegetables. Sauté shallots in butter until tender and add to sauce. Stir in Calvados and salt and pepper, if needed. Heat and pour sauce over tripe. Serve garnished with clusters of parsley.

VEAL

SAMPLE VEAL MENUS

Eggs in aspic*
*Blanquette of veal**
Fresh asparagus
Boston lettuce salad
Coeur à la crème*

Petite marmite*
*Saltimbocca**
Eggplant Parmigiana*
Tossed green salad
Fresh fruit compote with sour
   cream

Beef bouillon with vermicelli
*Veal scaloppine alla Marsala**
Spinach soufflé*
Tossed green salad
Zabaglione*

Eggs à la Russe*
*Veal à la Suisse**
Fresh broccoli
Céleri rémoulade*
Cheese fondue with green
   apples*

Antipasto*
*Veal Parmigiana**
Zucchini and tomatoes*
Sliced mushroom salad*
Zabaglione*

Prosciutto and melon*
*Veal and peppers**
Glazed carrots*
Tossed green salad
Dessert cheeses and espresso

Pâté de foie gras
*Wiener schnitzel**
Spinach soufflé*
Sliced mushroom salad*
Coffee Bavarian cream*

BLANQUETTE OF VEAL
MAKES 8 SERVINGS   6.1 GRAMS PER SERVING

3 pounds lean veal, 1½ inch cubes
1 quart water
1 teaspoon salt
1 medium onion, halved and stuck with 2 cloves
2 carrots, peeled and sliced
1 celery stalk with leaves, sliced
¼ teaspoon minced garlic
1 tablespoon chopped fresh parsley
20 peppercorns
¼ teaspoon thyme
1 bay leaf
16 small pearl onions, peeled
6 tablespoons butter or margarine
½ pound fresh mushrooms, sliced
½ teaspoon freshly grated nutmeg
Salt and freshly ground pepper
2 tablespoons flour
3 egg yolks, lightly beaten
1 cup heavy cream
1½ teaspoons fresh lemon juice
Chopped fresh parsley

Cover veal with water, bring to a boil, and simmer 10 minutes. Drain and rinse meat thoroughly under cold running water. Bring 1 quart of fresh salted water to a rapid boil in large kettle. Add veal, onion halves, carrots, celery, garlic, parsley, peppercorns, thyme, and bay leaf. Cover and simmer 1½ hours or until meat is tender when tested with a fork. Brown pearl onions in 2 tablespoons of butter. Add ¼ cup of water, cover, and simmer 20 minutes. Sauté mushrooms in 2 tablespoons of butter for 3 minutes. Sprinkle with nutmeg, salt, and pepper. Arrange veal, pearl onions, and mushrooms on heated platter. Keep warm.

Strain stock and discard vegetables. Bring to rapid boil and reduce liquid to 2 cups. Cream 2 tablespoons of butter with flour and stir into reduced stock. Boil for 1 minute or until sauce thickens. Combine egg yolks, cream, and lemon juice and slowly stir into sauce. Stir and simmer, without boiling, until sauce thickens again. Pour sauce over veal and sprinkle with chopped parsley.

SALTIMBOCCA

MAKES 8 SERVINGS 1.5 GRAMS PER SERVING

2 pounds veal cutlets, ¼ inch thick

8 slices prosciutto or boiled ham

8 fresh or ⅛ teaspoon dried sage leaves

2 tablespoons freshly grated imported Parmesan cheese

Freshly ground pepper

2 tablespoons melted butter or margarine

2 tablespoons olive or vegetable oil

½ cup Marsala wine

Trim and flatten cutlets between few layers of waxed paper with wooden mallet or rolling pin until ⅛ inch thick. Cover each cutlet with a slice of prosciutto. Add one sage leaf (or sprinkle very lightly with dried sage). Sprinkle lightly with Parmesan cheese and freshly ground pepper. Roll veal and secure each with toothpick. Sauté rolls slowly in butter and oil for 10 minutes or until browned on all sides. Add wine, cover, and simmer for 10 minutes or until meat is tender. Remove toothpicks, arrange rolls on heated platter and pour sauce over them.

VEAL SCALOPPINE ALLA MARSALA
MAKES 8 SERVINGS 1.4 GRAMS PER SERVING

2½ pounds veal cutlets, ½ inch thick
1 cup freshly grated imported Parmesan cheese
Salt and freshly ground pepper
1 garlic clove, halved
2 tablespoons olive or vegetable oil
½ cup strong beef bouillon
½ cup Marsala wine
1 tablespoon fresh lemon juice
⅛ teaspoon marjoram
⅛ teaspoon thyme

Sprinkle each cutlet generously with Parmesan cheese. Pound cheese into both sides of each cutlet with wooden mallet or rolling pin. Repeat until all cheese is used and cutlets are about ¼ inch thick. Sprinkle with salt and pepper and cut into 1-by-3-inch strips. Brown garlic in oil (discard garlic) and sauté strips until lightly browned on both sides. Add bouillon, wine, lemon juice, marjoram, and thyme. Cover and simmer 10 minutes or until veal is very tender. Transfer veal to heated platter. Bring liquid to a boil and reduce to 1 cup. Scrape sides and bottom of skillet and pour sauce over cutlets.

VEAL À LA SUISSE
MAKES 8 SERVINGS 5.6 GRAMS PER SERVING

2½ pounds veal tenderloin, ¼ inch thick
4 tablespoons butter or margarine
3 tablespoons minced shallots
1 pound fresh mushrooms, sliced
2 tablespoons flour
½ teaspoon paprika
¼ teaspoon grated lemon rind
1 teaspoon salt
¼ teaspoon freshly ground white pepper
½ cup dry white wine
1 cup heavy cream
1 teaspoon fresh lemon juice
Chopped fresh parsley

Cut veal into 1-inch squares, and sauté in 2 tablespoons of butter for 3 minutes or until meat is evenly browned. Set aside. Sauté shallots and mushrooms in 2 tablespoons of butter until tender and combine with veal. Sprinkle with flour, paprika, lemon rind, salt, and pepper. Stir in wine and cream. Simmer, without boiling, for 10 minutes. Stir in lemon juice and sprinkle with chopped parsley.

VEAL PARMIGIANA

MAKES 8 SERVINGS   .7 GRAM PER SERVING

2½ pounds veal cutlets, ¼ inch thick
Fresh lime juice
Salt and freshly ground pepper
¼ pound melted butter or margarine

1 cup freshly grated imported Parmesan cheese
2 eggs, lightly beaten
Lemon or lime wedges

Trim and flatten cutlets between few layers of waxed paper with wooden mallet or rolling pin until ⅛ inch thick. Brush cutlets with lime juice and sprinkle with salt and pepper. Dip into melted butter, then into grated cheese. Set aside for 20 minutes. Dip cutlets in lightly beaten eggs and again in grated cheese. Sprinkle with remaining cheese and refrigerate for 2 hours. Sauté cheese-coated cutlets in remaining melted butter for 2 minutes on each side until golden brown. Serve garnished with lemon or lime wedges.

VEAL AND PEPPERS

MAKES 8 SERVINGS   4.4 GRAMS PER SERVING

2½ pounds veal tenderloin,
   ¼ inch thick
3 tablespoons olive or
   vegetable oil
3 green peppers, seeded and
   cut into eighths
¼ cup minced shallots
⅛ teaspoon crushed garlic
½ teaspoon salt

¼ teaspoon freshly ground
   pepper
1 cup peeled, diced tomatoes,
   fresh or canned
½ cup freshly grated
   Parmesan cheese
Chopped fresh tarragon or
   Italian parsley

Cut veal into 3-by-¾-inch strips and sauté in oil for 3 minutes or until meat is evenly browned. Stir in green peppers, shallots, garlic, salt, and pepper and simmer 10 minutes. Stir in tomatoes and cheese, cover and simmer 10 minutes or until peppers are tender. Garnish with chopped tarragon or Italian parsley.

WIENER SCHNITZEL

MAKES 8 SERVINGS   7.4 GRAMS PER SERVING

2½ pounds veal cutlets, ¼ inch
   thick
¼ cup fresh lemon juice
Salt and freshly ground pepper
2 eggs, lightly beaten
2 tablespoons dry white wine
   or water
¾ cup fine bread crumbs

3 tablespoons flour
½ pound butter or margarine
8 thin lemon slices
8 slices hard-cooked eggs
8 small anchovy fillet rolls
Capers
Paprika

Trim and flatten cutlets flat between few layers of waxed paper with wooden mallet or rolling pin until ⅛ inch thick. Marinate veal in lemon juice for 1 hour. Drain, dry cutlets thoroughly, and sprinkle both sides with salt and pepper. Combine eggs and wine. Combine bread crumbs and flour. Dip cutlets into egg mixture and then into bread crumb mixture. Set aside for 30 minutes or longer.

Melt butter until it foams. Reduce heat and sauté veal 1½ minutes on each side or until golden brown. Drain on paper towels and place on heated platter. Garnish cutlets with lemon slices topped with sliced hard-cooked eggs, anchovy rolls, and capers. Sprinkle with paprika.

Sauces

Very low carbohydrate sauces may sound like a laughable contradiction, but much to the surprise of those who've eaten mine, it's perfectly possible to enjoy creamy-tasting sauces and eliminate the usual high carbohydrate content. The major difference is only a matter of thickness. Very low carbohydrate sauces are prepared with a minimum of flour or no flour at all. Low carbohydrate sauces actually taste much better in my opinion, for they *enhance* the flavor of whatever they accompany rather than masking it.

Your electric blender has changed sauce cookery from a tiresome, testy chore to an easy delight. The blended Hollandaise sauce, for example, actually can be successfully frozen and reheated if you don't let it come to a boil. Use a double boiler when reheating all egg-yolk-thickened sauces and soups as they will curdle or separate if exposed to too much heat.

The beginning of the recipe for every one of the twenty-seven superb sauces described in this book tells what dishes the sauce best enhances.

If you serve sauce with your entrée, don't put sauce on your vegetable, and vice versa. Think of your meal in terms of total texture, color, richness, and variety of taste sensations.

BROWN SAUCES

BROWN SAUCE

MAKES 3 CUPS   .4 GRAM PER TABLESPOON

For soups, stews, or as a base for other sauces

2½ cups strong beef bouillon
3 tablespoons chopped onions
3 tablespoons chopped peeled carrots
1 tablespoon chopped celery
½ cup dry red wine

1 tablespoon chopped fresh parsley
⅓ bay leaf
⅛ teaspoon thyme
1 tablespoon tomato purée
2 tablespoons arrowroot or cornstarch

Simmer beef bouillon and remaining ingredients (except arrowroot) for 30 to 40 minutes. Strain liquid through fine sieve and discard vegetables. Make a paste of ¼ cup of bouillon and arrowroot and stir into sauce. Simmer 5 minutes or until thickened.

SAUCE PÉRIGUEUX
MAKES 3 CUPS   .4 GRAM PER TABLESPOON

For beef, chicken, or veal

3 cups brown sauce   2 tablespoons cold butter
1 small can truffles

Heat brown sauce and stir in liquid from truffles. Chop half of truffles, stir into sauce, and bring to a rapid boil. Remove pan from heat and stir in cold butter cut into small pieces. Slice remaining truffles and use as garnish.

WHITE SAUCES

BÉCHAMEL SAUCE (WHITE SAUCE)
MAKES 1¼ CUPS   .9 GRAM PER TABLESPOON

For chicken, egg, fish, mushroom dishes, or as a base for other sauces

1½ tablespoons softened butter
　　or margarine
1½ tablespoons all-purpose
　　flour
　1 cup hot milk

Pinch of nutmeg
Pinch of thyme
Salt and freshly ground white
　　pepper

Blend all ingredients in electric blender at high speed for 10 seconds. Cook sauce over very low heat for 3 minutes, stirring occasionally.

CHEESE SAUCE
MAKES 1¾ CUPS   .7 GRAM PER TABLESPOON

For eggs or vegetables au gratin

1¼ cups Béchamel sauce
¼ teaspoon dry mustard

½ cup diced sharp Cheddar
　　cheese
Dash of paprika

Blend all ingredients in electric blender at high speed for 10 seconds. Scrape down sides of blender with rubber spatula and blend again for 5 seconds. Cook sauce over very low heat for 3 minutes, stirring occasionally.

MORNAY SAUCE

MAKES 1½ CUPS .8 GRAM PER TABLESPOON

For chicken, eggs, fish, or vegetables

1¼ cups Béchamel sauce
  2 teaspoons chicken stock
    concentrate
  2 tablespoons diced Gruyère
    cheese

2 tablespoons diced
  Parmesan cheese
2 egg yolks

Blend all ingredients in electric blender at high speed for 10 seconds. Scrape down sides of blender with rubber spatula and blend again for 5 seconds. Cook sauce over very low heat for 3 minutes, stirring occasionally.

SAUCE VELOUTÉ (WHITE SAUCE)

MAKES 1¼ CUPS .5 GRAM PER TABLESPOON

For calves' brains, chicken, eggs, fish, or as a base for other sauces

2 tablespoons softened butter
  or margarine
2 tablespoons all-purpose flour

1 cup hot chicken or fish broth
Salt and freshly ground white
  pepper

Blend all ingredients in electric blender at high speed for 10 seconds. Cook sauce over very low heat for 3 minutes, stirring occasionally.

ALLEMANDE SAUCE
MAKES 2 CUPS .5 GRAM PER TABLESPOON

For chicken, fish, or vegetables

1¼ cups sauce Velouté
½ cup heavy cream
2 egg yolks
½ teaspoon fresh lemon juice

1½ tablespoons freshly grated
Parmesan cheese
Freshly grated nutmeg

Blend all ingredients in electric blender at high speed for 10 seconds. Cook sauce over very low heat for 3 minutes, stirring occasionally.

BUTTER SAUCES

ALMOND BUTTER
MAKES 1 CUP .6 GRAM PER TABLESPOON

For chicken, seafood, or vegetables

¼ pound butter or margarine
½ cup slivered almonds
1 teaspoon chopped chives
    (optional)

1 teaspoon fresh lemon juice
    (optional)
Freshly grated nutmeg
Salt and freshly ground white
    pepper

Heat butter until foaming, stir in almonds and lightly brown them. Add remaining ingredients and spoon almonds (not butter) over chicken, seafood, or vegetables.

BEURRE NOIR—BLACK BUTTER
MAKES 1 CUP .3 GRAM PER TABLESPOON

For brains, fish, meat, or vegetables

¾ cup (1½ sticks) butter
3 tablespoons minced parsley

4 tablespoons white wine
    vinegar or fresh lemon juice
Salt and freshly ground pepper

Cut butter into pieces and melt over low heat. Skim off scum as it foams on top and strain clear yellow portion (clarified butter). Discard milky sediment (whey). Rinse out pan and heat clarified butter slowly until it turns golden nut brown. Stir in parsley and set aside.

Bring vinegar or lemon juice to a boil, reduce to 1 tablespoon and add to clarified butter. Reheat when ready to use.

GARLIC BUTTER
MAKES ½ CUP   .3 GRAM PER TABLESPOON

For grilled meats or bread

¼ pound softened butter or
   margarine
1 teaspoon minced garlic
¼ teaspoon crushed dried

thyme, dill, or tarragon
   (optional)
Salt and freshly ground white
   pepper

Combine all ingredients and blend well. Set aside for 1 hour before using.

LEMON BUTTER
MAKES ½ CUP   .2 GRAM PER TABLESPOON

For artichokes or lobster

¼ pound sweet butter or
   margarine
2 tablespoons fresh lemon
   juice

2 drops Tabasco sauce
¼ teaspoon salt

Slowly melt butter so it does not brown and stir in remaining ingredients.

MAÎTRE D'HÔTEL BUTTER
MAKES ¾ CUP   .3 GRAM PER TABLESPOON

For broiled liver, grilled meats, or fish

¼ pound softened butter or
  margarine
2 tablespoons minced parsley

2 tablespoons minced chives
2 tablespoons fresh lemon
  juice

Cream butter with parsley and chives and gradually stir in lemon juice. Roll butter mixture in a piece of plastic wrap and refrigerate to harden. Slice before serving.

MEUNIÈRE BUTTER
MAKES ½ CUP   .2 GRAM PER TABLESPOON

For brook trout, seafood, or vegetables

¼ pound sweet butter or
  margarine
2 teaspoons fresh lemon juice

1 tablespoon minced fresh
  parsley

Melt butter very slowly until it turns nut brown. Stir in lemon juice and pour over seafood or vegetables. Sprinkle with parsley and serve.

CREAM SAUCES

DRESDEN SAUCE
MAKES 1 CUP   .5 GRAM PER TABLESPOON

For beef fondue, broiled fish, or smoked trout

½ teaspoon prepared horseradish
1 cup sour cream

½ teaspoon prepared hot mustard (Dijon or Düsseldorf)
¼ teaspoon salt
Freshly ground white pepper

Thoroughly drain horseradish and combine with remaining ingredients. Serve chilled.

EPICUREAN SAUCE
MAKES 1½ CUPS   .3 GRAM PER TABLESPOON

For beef fondue, ham, roast beef, or tongue

1 teaspoon fresh lemon juice
½ teaspoon prepared hot mustard (Dijon or Düsseldorf)
3 tablespoons mayonnaise
2 tablespoons prepared horseradish

¼ teaspoon salt
⅛ teaspoon paprika
Cayenne pepper
½ cup heavy cream

125

Combine all ingredients except cream. At serving time, whip cream until stiff and fold into combined ingredients. Serve immediately.

LOBSTER SAUCE

MAKES 3 CUPS .5 GRAM PER TABLESPOON

For eggs, deviled crab, or fish

1 tablespoon minced shallots	½ cup milk
1 tablespoon butter or margarine	1 cup diced cooked lobster
1 tablespoon flour	2 tablespoons sherry
¾ cup V-8 juice	½ cup heavy cream

Sauté shallots in butter until tender. Sprinkle with flour and stir in V-8 juice and milk. Bring to a boil and simmer 1 minute, stirring constantly until smooth and thickened. Stir in lobster (shrimp or crab meat may be substituted), sherry, and cream. Reheat without boiling.

MUSTARD SAUCE

MAKES 1¼ CUPS .5 GRAM PER TABLESPOON

For beef, beef fondue, fish, or ham

1 cup sour cream	Salt and freshly ground pepper
3 tablespoons hot prepared mustard (Dijon or Düsseldorf)	1 egg yolk, lightly beaten

Combine sour cream, mustard, salt, and pepper. Stir in egg yolk and simmer until thickened. Chill.

SHRIMP SAUCE

MAKES 2½ CUPS   .3 GRAM PER TABLESPOON

For baked oysters, deviled crab, or fish

2 tablespoons softened butter
  or margarine
1 tablespoon flour
½ teaspoon salt
Freshly ground white pepper
¼ cup dry white wine
¾ cup chicken broth

2 egg yolks, lightly beaten
1 teaspoon lemon juice
1 cup cooked shrimp, cut in
  pieces
¼ cup freshly grated Parmesan
  cheese

Blend butter, flour, salt, and pepper and melt over very low heat, stirring until smooth. Simmer 2 minutes without browning. Slowly stir in wine and broth. Cool slightly. Combine egg yolks and lemon juice with some sauce and stir into sauce. Stir in shrimp (crab or lobster meat may be substituted) and cheese. Simmer, without boiling, for 2 minutes or until sauce thickens. Reheat without boiling.

HOLLANDAISE BASE SAUCES

HOLLANDAISE SAUCE

MAKES 1¾ CUPS   .3 GRAM PER TABLESPOON

For chicken, eggs, fish, veal, or vegetables

6 egg yolks	Cayenne pepper
¼ cup fresh lemon juice	½ pound melted butter or
½ teaspoon salt	margarine

Combine egg yolks, lemon juice, salt, and cayenne in electric blender. Cover. Melt butter slowly to prevent browning. Turn blender on low speed, remove cover, and pour in hot butter. Turn blender off immediately and serve.

BÉARNAISE SAUCE

MAKES 1¾ CUPS   .3 GRAM PER TABLESPOON

For beef fondue, broiled meats, chicken, or vegetables

¼ cup dry white wine	1 tablespoon chopped
2 tablespoons tarragon wine	scallions
vinegar	10 peppercorns
1 tablespoon chopped fresh	1¾ cups Hollandaise sauce
or 2 teaspoons dried	
tarragon	

128

Boil wine, vinegar, tarragon, scallions, and peppercorns until most of liquid has evaporated. Discard peppercorns. Pour mixture into hot Hollandaise sauce in electric blender and blend for 5 seconds.

HORSERADISH MOUSSELINE SAUCE
MAKES 2 CUPS .3 GRAM PER TABLESPOON

For eggs, fish, salmon mousse, or vegetables

1 tablespoon prepared horseradish

1 cup Hollandaise sauce
½ cup heavy cream

Stir horseradish into Hollandaise sauce. Whip cream until stiff and carefully fold in half of Hollandaise sauce mixture so as not to break down whipped cream. Carefully fold in remaining Hollandaise sauce mixture. Serve immediately.

MAYONNAISE BASE SAUCES

CURRY SAUCE
MAKES 1 CUP .4 GRAM PER TABLESPOON

For beef fondue, fruit salad, or seafood

1 cup mayonnaise

1 tablespoon tomato paste
2 teaspoons curry powder

Mix all ingredients thoroughly and chill.

SAUCE RAVIGOTE
MAKES 2 CUPS .3 GRAM PER TABLESPOON

For fish or mussels

2 tablespoons chopped shallots
2 tablespoons drained chopped capers
2 tablespoons chopped fresh parsley
1 tablespoon chopped fresh or 1 teaspoon dried tarragon

½ cup dry white wine or reduced stock
1 teaspoon lemon juice
1 cup mayonnaise
1 tablespoon prepared hot mustard (Dijon or Düsseldorf)
1 hard-cooked egg

Bring shallots, capers, parsley, tarragon, wine (or stock), and lemon juice to a boil, lower heat, and simmer 15 minutes. Pour into electric blender. Add mayonnaise and mustard, cover and blend at high speed for 3 seconds. Scrape sides of blender with rubber spatula. Cover and blend again for 5 seconds. Push hard-cooked egg onto blender blades with rubber spatula and blend at medium speed for 3 seconds.

RÉMOULADE SAUCE

MAKES 1¼ CUPS .2 GRAM PER TABLESPOON

For fried fish, or seafood cocktails

1 cup mayonnaise
2 hard-cooked egg yolks
2 tablespoons hot prepared
  mustard (Dijon or Düsseldorf)
1 teaspoon fresh lemon juice

1 teaspoon chopped fresh or
  ½ teaspoon dried tarragon
1 teaspoon chopped fresh
  parsley
1 tablespoon capers, drained
  (optional)

Blend all ingredients (except capers) in electric blender at high speed for 6 seconds. Occasionally scrape sides of blender with rubber spatula. Chill before serving. Add capers, if desired.

SEAFOOD SAUCE

MAKES 2 CUPS .4 GRAM PER TABLESPOON

For crab meat, lobster, or shrimp cocktail

1 cup mayonnaise
½ cup cottage cheese
⅓ cup sliced onions
¼ teaspoon chopped garlic
1 teaspoon chili sauce
2 teaspoons Worcestershire
  sauce
1 teaspoon dry sherry

2 drops Tabasco sauce
1 teaspoon dry mustard
¼ teaspoon caraway seeds
¼ teaspoon celery salt
¼ teaspoon salt
¼ teaspoon freshly ground
  pepper

Blend all ingredients in electric blender for 20 seconds at high speed. Occasionally scrape sides of blender with rubber spatula. Refrigerate overnight and serve chilled.

TARTAR SAUCE

MAKES 1¼ CUPS .3 GRAM PER TABLESPOON

For beef fondue, fried fish, or shellfish

1 cup mayonnaise
1 tablespoon chopped gherkin
  pickles
1 teaspoon chopped onions
2 pitted green olives, chopped

1 tablespoon chopped fresh
  parsley
1 tablespoon chopped chives
1 teaspoon chopped tarragon
Salt and freshly ground white
  pepper

Blend all ingredients in electric blender at low speed for 5 seconds. Scrape sides of blender with rubber spatula and blend again for 3 seconds. Serve at room temperature.

SAUCE VERTE

MAKES 1¾ CUPS .2 GRAM PER TABLESPOON

For beef fondue, smoked fish, salads, or cold salmon

3 egg yolks
2 tablespoons cream
1 tablespoon fresh lemon juice
1 tablespoon tarragon wine
  vinegar
2 tablespoons chopped spinach
  leaves
2 tablespoons chopped
  watercress leaves

1 tablespoon chopped fresh
  tarragon or dill
1 tablespoon chopped chives
½ teaspoon dry mustard
½ teaspoon salt
Cayenne pepper
¾ cup olive or corn oil

Blend all ingredients in electric blender (except oil) at low speed for 5 seconds. Scrape sides of blender with rubber spatula. Cover blender and blend at low speed again. Immediately remove cover and pour in oil in slow steady stream. Turn motor off immediately. Chill before serving.

Egg Dishes

Eggs are a great buy for your protein dollar! And they are very low in carbohydrate content, while high in many other valuable nutrients. The variations possible in egg preparation are truly infinite, and there's no question that an omelet is a cook's best friend—you can do just about anything with it. You can prepare it with fine herbs, spinach, mushrooms, parsley, leftovers, or just about any other combination your palate tells you will be delicious. You can extend a handful of more expensive protein by combining your omelet with cheese, meats, or seafood, and enjoy their flavor at a fraction of what they would cost if they were the mainstay of the meal.

Soufflés can serve the same purpose, and, although they must be served instantly or they will collapse, they can be prepared ahead. Once a soufflé is mixed, you can put it in a warm area protected from drafts, and it will last an hour before you need cook it. No longer, though!

Quiche Lorraine sounds formidable—but it's not, and you can incorporate meat, cheese, seafood, and vegetables in it the way you can in an omelet or soufflé.

What follows are some delicious, truly filling egg dishes you can serve at any hour from breakfast through supper.

SAMPLE EGG DISH MENUS

Cheese soufflé*
Crisp fresh spinach salad
Cantaloupe melon with lemon
    wedges

Omelet chasseur*
Hearts of palm salad*
Honeydew melon

Jellied chicken consommé
Eggs Florentine*
Sliced fresh mushroom salad*
Casaba melon

Jellied Madrilène with lemon
    wedge

*Eggs à la Russe on artichoke
    bottoms**
Crisp fresh spinach salad
Persian melon

Quiche Lorraine*
Endive and watercress salad
Fresh strawberries and mandarin
    orange sections

CHEESE SOUFFLÉ

MAKES 8 SERVINGS 6.7 GRAMS PER SERVING

3½ tablespoons softened butter or margarine	1 teaspoon salt
⅓ cup sifted flour	Cayenne pepper
1½ cups milk	½ pound natural sharp Cheddar cheese
⅛ teaspoon Worcestershire sauce	6 eggs, separated
	2 egg whites

Blend butter and flour. Melt over very low heat and stir with wooden spoon until smooth. Simmer 2 minutes without browning. Bring milk, Worcestershire sauce, salt, and cayenne to a boil and stir vigorously into butter mixture. Cool for 3 minutes. Finely grate cheese into milk mixture, heat, and stir until it melts. Beat in egg yolks one at a time. Cook and stir for 1 minute or until egg yolks thicken. Set aside and cool.

Preheat oven to 375° F. Beat egg whites until stiff, but not dry, and fold into cheese mixture. Pour into eight individual 1½-cup soufflé dishes (greased or ungreased, as desired). Set soufflé dishes in pan of boiling water and bake 15 to 20 minutes, or until top is delicately browned and puffed. Serve immediately while piping hot and still puffed.

EGGS À LA RUSSE ON ARTICHOKE BOTTOMS

MAKES 8 SERVINGS 5.8 GRAMS PER SERVING

8 hard-cooked eggs	1 tablespoon light cream
8 large artichoke bottoms	Sliced truffles
1 cup Hollandaise sauce (see *Sauces*)	

Carefully peel hard-cooked eggs and cut in half lengthwise. Arrange two halves, cut side down, on top of each artichoke bottom on individual serving plates. Combine Hollandaise sauce with cream and pour over eggs. Serve garnished with sliced truffles.

EGGS FLORENTINE
MAKES 8 SERVINGS   4.1 GRAMS PER SERVING

8 thin slices cooked ham	Freshly grated nutmeg
2 tablespoons butter or margarine	Salt and freshly ground pepper
3 tablespoons freshly grated Parmesan cheese	16 poached eggs
	1¾ cups Hollandaise sauce (see *Sauces*)
3 cups cooked chopped spinach, frozen or fresh	Truffles, sliced

Sauté ham slices in butter on both sides and place on heated individual plates. Stir Parmesan cheese into spinach seasoned with nutmeg, salt, and pepper and heat through. Spoon equal portions on top of ham slices. Place 2 poached eggs on each bed of spinach and cover with Hollandaise sauce. Garnish with sliced truffles and serve.

OMELET CHASSEUR
MAKES 8 SERVINGS   3.5 GRAMS PER SERVING

4 chicken livers, quartered	Salt and freshly ground pepper
5 tablespoons butter or margarine	¼ cup strong beef bouillon
2½ teaspoons chopped scallions including greens	2 tablespoons dry white wine
	8 3-egg omelets
4 fresh mushrooms, sliced	2 dozen small fresh mushroom caps
2 teaspoons flour	Chopped fresh parsley

Sauté livers in 2 tablespoons of butter for 7 minutes or until tender. Set livers aside. Add 1 tablespoon of butter to skillet and sauté scallions 1 minute. Stir in sliced mushrooms and sauté for 2 minutes. Sprinkle with flour, salt, and pepper. Stir in bouillon and wine. Stir and simmer until mixture thickens. Add chicken livers and keep warm while making omelets. Sauté mushroom caps for 2 minutes in 2 tablespoons of butter. Fill omelets with hot liver mixture. Garnish with mushroom caps and sprinkle with parsley.

QUICHE LORRAINE

MAKES 8 SERVINGS 2.9 GRAMS PER SERVING

5 slices crisp bacon, diced	2 cups cream
¼ cup minced onions	¼ teaspoon freshly grated
1 teaspoon chopped chives	nutmeg
1 cup diced imported Gruyère	Cayenne pepper
cheese	½ teaspoon salt
¼ cup freshly grated imported	¼ teaspoon freshly ground
Parmesan cheese	white pepper
4 eggs, lightly beaten	

Sauté bacon until crisp. Drain and set aside. Pour off all but 1 tablespoon of bacon drippings and sauté onions until tender. Sprinkle bacon, onions, chives and cheeses evenly over bottom of Teflon-lined pie pan. Combine eggs, cream, nutmeg, cayenne, salt, and pepper and strain over all.

Preheat oven to 375° F. Bake quiche in lower third of oven for 25 to 30 minutes or until puffed and browned. A knife stuck into center should come out clean. Serve piping hot as an appetizer or main luncheon course.

Vegetables

Many vegetables are surprisingly high in carbohydrate content and don't fit into my bill of fare. The interesting thing about vegetables high in carbohydrates is that you can actually taste the starch or sugar in those that are high on the gram counter.

Contrast the taste of potatoes, rice, lima beans, peas, and corn with the flavor of spinach, broccoli, zucchini, asparagus, cauliflower, green beans, eggplant, and mushrooms. The latter are all extremely low in carbohydrate—and tasting them tells you that; there is no "thick," mealy, or sweet taste to them. In my opinion, the latter also have much better, more striking textures, shapes, and interesting, individual flavors than the former.

Vegetables too often suffer from unimaginative cooking. No matter how you serve them they must not be cooked too much in advance or they become watery and lose their lovely fresh color, flavor, shape, and much of their nutritional value.

Don't hesitate to use good frozen vegetables. They are so convenient and are quite respectable. Simply treat them as if they were fresh or add some touches of your own to individualize them, such as a pinch of dill in frozen green beans or a dash of nutmeg in frozen spinach.

ASPARAGUS WITH HOLLANDAISE
MAKES 8 SERVINGS   3.7 GRAMS PER SERVING

4 pounds fresh young
   asparagus
½ teaspoon salt

1¾ cups Hollandaise sauce
    (see *Sauces*)

Remove tough ends of asparagus stalks. Wash carefully, using a vegetable brush, if necessary, to remove all sand and grit. Tie asparagus into 8 serving bunches. Stand bunches upright in bottom of double boiler in 1 inch of boiling water. Cover with inverted top of double boiler and steam 12 minutes or until tender but still firm. Serve piping hot with Hollandaise sauce (or mornay sauce or beurre noir).

BEETS WITH ORANGE SAUCE
MAKES 8 SERVINGS   7.8 GRAMS PER SERVING

2 pounds small young beets,
   fresh or canned
½ teaspoon cornstarch
⅓ cup fresh orange juice
1 teaspoon fresh lemon juice
4 tablespoons coarsely
   chopped walnuts

1 tablespoon grated orange
   rind
½ teaspoon salt
2 tablespoons butter or
   margarine

Wash fresh beets under cold water and cut off all but 1 inch of stem leaving root intact. Half cover beets with boiling water, cover, and boil 30 minutes or until tender. Drain and plunge into cold water. When cool enough to handle, cut off stem and slip off skin and root end with fingers. With an egg slicer, cut beets into thin slices.

Dissolve cornstarch in orange juice. Add lemon juice and walnuts and bring to a boil. Stir until sauce is clear. Stir in beets, orange rind, and salt. At serving time, dot with butter and heat slowly.

BROCCOLI ALLEMANDE

MAKES 8 SERVINGS   5.3 GRAMS PER SERVING

2 pounds young broccoli spears	4 tablespoons freshly grated Parmesan cheese
½ teaspoon salt	Chopped chives or parsley
1 cup Allemande sauce (see Sauces)	

Remove large coarse leaves and tough lower part of broccoli stalks. Cut stalks in half or quarters depending on size. Stand broccoli upright in 1 inch of boiling water, cover, and simmer 10 minutes or until tender but still firm. Drain and transfer to ovenproof serving platter. Sprinkle with salt. Pour Allemande sauce over broccoli, sprinkle with grated cheese, and brown under broiler. Sprinkle with chives and serve piping hot.

BRUSSELS SPROUTS SAUTÉ

MAKES 8 SERVINGS 7.0 GRAMS PER SERVING

1½ pounds young Brussels
    sprouts, fresh or frozen
2 eggs, lightly beaten
2 tablespoons milk
2 tablespoons sherry

2 teaspoons grated onion
½ teaspoon salt
¼ cup fine bread crumbs
¼ cup minced salted peanuts
¼ pound butter or margarine

Remove tough or wilted outer leaves of fresh Brussels sprouts. Cut off stems and cut small x in each stem end. Drop fresh Brussels sprouts into 1 inch of boiling water, cover and simmer 10 minutes or until tender but still firm. Combine eggs, milk, sherry, onion, and salt. Combine bread crumbs and peanuts. Dip drained sprouts in egg mixture, then roll in peanut mixture and set aside for 20 minutes. Sauté sprouts in butter until lightly browned on all sides and serve.

GLAZED CARROTS

MAKES 8 SERVINGS 5.8 GRAMS PER SERVING

3 cans imported Belgian
    carrots, drained
3 tablespoons butter or
    margarine

1 teaspoon sugar
½ teaspoon salt
1½ tablespoons minced chives

Cut off stem ends from tiny Belgian carrots, if necessary. Melt butter and sugar and simmer until butter caramelizes but does not brown. Add carrots, sprinkle with salt, and sauté 5 minutes. Roll carrots so evenly coated and glazed. Sprinkle with chopped chives and serve.

CAULIFLOWER AU GRATIN

MAKES 8 SERVINGS 5.0 GRAMS PER SERVING

1 large head of cauliflower
Salt
2 tablespoons freshly grated
Parmesan cheese

1¾ cups cheese sauce (see
Sauces)
Chopped chives or fresh parsley

Wash and remove green outer leaves. Cut out center core.
Place cauliflower, core side down, on trivet in 1 inch of boiling
water. Cover and steam 20 to 25 minutes or until tender but
still firm. Place on heated platter and sprinkle lightly with salt
and Parmesan cheese. Pour hot cheese sauce over cauliflower
and garnish with chopped chives.

BRAISED CELERY

MAKES 8 SERVINGS 3.6 GRAMS PER SERVING

8 celery hearts, halved
lengthwise
1½ cups strong beef bouillon
2 tablespoons minced onions

2 tablespoons butter or
margarine
2 tablespoons flour
Chopped fresh tarragon or
chives
Paprika

Discard older leaves. Bring celery and bouillon to a boil,
cover, and simmer for 10 minutes or until tender but still
crisp. Drain and reserve 1 cup of bouillon. Keep warm. Sauté
onions in butter until tender. Sprinkle with flour, stir in bouillon, and bring to a boil. Simmer until thickened, stirring occasionally. Pour thickened bouillon over celery and heat through.
Sprinkle with tarragon and paprika and serve.

EGGPLANT PARMIGIANA
MAKES 8 SERVINGS   7.3 GRAMS PER SERVING

½ cup olive or vegetable oil
2 teaspoons grated onion
½ teaspoon minced garlic
1 teaspoon salt
1 large unpeeled eggplant,
   ½-inch slices
2½ cups peeled chopped Italian
   tomatoes, fresh or canned

½ teaspoon oregano
Freshly grated nutmeg
1 cup freshly grated imported
   Parmesan cheese
Salt and freshly ground pepper
½ pound mozzarella cheese,
   thinly sliced

Combine oil, onion, garlic, and salt. Dip sliced eggplant in oil and place on greased baking sheet. Broil slices 4 inches from heat for 5 minutes, brushing once with oil mixture. Turn, brush again with oil, and broil 2 minutes or until tender. Combine tomatoes, oregano, nutmeg, ¾ cup of Parmesan cheese, salt, and pepper. Spread a third of tomatoes, half of eggplant, and mozzarella cheese slices in well-buttered casserole. Repeat layers, ending with tomato sauce, and sprinkle with remaining Parmesan cheese. Preheat oven to 350° F. and bake 30 minutes or until nicely browned and bubbling.

BRAISED BELGIAN ENDIVE
MAKES 8 SERVINGS   5.0 GRAMS PER SERVING

16 small young Belgian endive
4 tablespoons butter or
   margarine
Freshly ground white pepper

¼ teaspoon dried sweet basil
½ cup strong beef bouillon
½ cup coursely chopped
   English walnuts

Wash endive and discard any wilted leaves. Cut off some root end of each endive. Melt 2 tablespoons of butter in large skillet and arrange endive in single layer. Sprinkle very lightly with white pepper and basil. Add bouillon, cover and simmer 10 minutes or until tender but still firm. Add more bouillon, if necessary. Sauté walnuts in 2 tablespoons of butter until lightly browned. Carefully remove endive to heated platter and sprinkle with walnuts.

GREEN BEANS WITH MUSHROOMS
MAKES 8 SERVINGS   6.0 GRAMS PER SERVING

2 pounds green beans, fresh
  or frozen
Dried dill weed
4 tablespoons butter or
  margarine
½ teaspoon salt

Freshly ground pepper
½ pound sliced fresh
  mushrooms
½ teaspoon fresh lemon juice
Freshly grated nutmeg
1 cup sour cream

Wash fresh green beans, string, snap off ends, and cut lengthwise. Stir into a ½ inch of boiling water sprinkled with dill and simmer 15 minutes or until tender but still firm. Drain and add 2 tablespoons of butter, salt, and pepper. Sauté mushrooms in 2 tablespoons of butter for 3 minutes or until tender. Sprinkle with lemon juice and nutmeg. Combine green beans, mushrooms, and sour cream. Stir and heat without boiling.

MUSHROOMS UNDER GLASS
MAKES 8 SERVINGS   6.2 GRAMS PER SERVING

2 pounds fresh mushroom caps
¼ pound softened butter or
  margarine
1 tablespoon fresh lemon juice
2 tablespoons chopped fresh
  parsley

⅛ teaspoon marjoram
½ teaspoon salt
¼ teaspoon paprika
1 cup cream
3 tablespoons sherry
Fresh parsley clusters

Wipe each mushroom cap clean. Cream butter with lemon juice, parsley, marjoram, salt, and paprika and spread in mushroom caps. Arrange mushroom caps in large baking dish, smooth side down, and pour cream on top. Cover tightly with a glass dome or bowl. Preheat oven to 375° F. Bake mushrooms 25 minutes, adding more cream if mushrooms become dry. Just before serving, stir in sherry and garnish with parsley clusters.

CHINESE SNOW PEAS

MAKES 8 SERVINGS   5.2 GRAMS PER SERVING

1 pound fresh Chinese snow peas
3 tablespoons peanut or vegetable oil
1 teaspoon soy sauce
1 teaspoon salt
¾ cup chicken broth
½ teaspoon arrowroot
1 tablespoon water
½ cup sliced water chestnuts
½ cup sliced bamboo shoots

Remove tips and strings from fresh snow peas. Wash and drain thoroughly. Heat oil in large skillet and stir in snow peas. Cook 1 minute over high heat, tossing constantly. Sprinkle with soy sauce and salt. Stir in chicken broth, cover and simmer 3 minutes or until peas are tender but still firm. Remove peas to heated dish. Blend arrowroot and water and stir into broth. Add water chestnuts and bamboo shoots and simmer until sauce thickens, not more than 1 minute. Pour sauce over snow peas and serve piping hot.

SPINACH SOUFFLÉ

MAKES 8 SERVINGS   5.6 GRAMS PER SERVING

2 tablespoons chopped onions
4 tablespoons butter or margarine
2 cups cooked chopped spinach, drained
¼ cup sifted flour
1 cup heavy cream
1 cup chicken broth
6 egg yolks
⅛ teaspoon freshly grated nutmeg
1 cup freshly grated Parmesan cheese
1 teaspoon salt
⅛ teaspoon freshly ground white pepper
6 egg whites

Sauté onions in 1 tablespoon of butter until tender. Add spinach, 3 tablespoons of butter, flour, cream, broth, egg yolks, nutmeg, ¾ cup of Parmesan cheese, salt, and pepper to electric blender. Cover and blend at high speed 15 seconds. Scrape sides with rubber spatula and blend again. Pour into saucepan and simmer 1 minute. Stir until thickened. Set aside to cool.

Preheat oven to 325° F. Generously butter an 8-cup soufflé dish or eight individual soufflé ramekins and dust with Parmesan cheese. Beat egg whites until stiff but not dry. Fold and cut them into spinach mixture and spoon into soufflé dish or ramekins. Sprinkle with remaining Parmesan cheese. Set soufflé dish or ramekins in shallow pan of hot water in center of oven. Bake soufflé 25 to 30 minutes and ramekins 12 to 15 minutes or until firm. Serve immediately.

BAKED STUFFED TOMATOES

MAKES 8 SERVINGS 7.1 GRAMS PER SERVING

8 firm ripe tomatoes	5 tablespoons butter or
½ teaspoon crushed dried basil,	margarine
oregano, or thyme	1 tablespoon fresh lemon juice
Salt and freshly ground pepper	2 egg yolks, lightly beaten
¾ pound chopped fresh	2 tablespoons cream
mushrooms	Fresh parsley or watercress
	clusters

Cut off stem end of each tomato, scoop out seeds, and invert to drain 15 minutes. Sprinkle insides with basil, salt, and pepper. Sauté mushrooms in 3 tablespoons of butter 3 minutes or until tender. Sprinkle lightly with lemon juice, salt, and pepper. Combine egg yolks and cream and stir into mushrooms. Fill each tomato with mushroom mixture and dot with remaining butter. Place in shallow baking dish with enough water to prevent scorching. Preheat oven to 350° F. Bake 10 minutes or until thoroughly heated but still firm. Garnish with clusters of parsley or watercress and serve.

BROILED TOMATOES

MAKES 8 SERVINGS   4.5 GRAMS PER SERVING

4 large firm ripe tomatoes
3 tablespoons tarragon wine
  vinegar
4 teaspoons minced onions

2 teaspoons crushed dried
  oregano
3 tablespoons butter or
  margarine
Salt and freshly ground pepper

Drop tomatoes into boiling water for 10 seconds, drain and peel. Cut in half crosswise. Sprinkle with vinegar, onions, oregano, salt, and pepper and dot liberally with butter. Refrigerate 1 hour or longer. Preheat broiler. Place tomatoes on buttered shallow baking dish and broil 5 to 7 minutes or until thoroughly heated but still firm.

STUFFED ZUCCHINI

MAKES 8 SERVINGS   3.4 GRAMS PER SERVING

8 small zucchini
1 tablespoon minced onions
1 tablespoon olive or
  vegetable oil
1¼ cups chopped mushrooms
½ cup freshly grated Parmesan
  or Gruyère cheese

⅛ teaspoon marjoram, sweet
  basil, or thyme
Salt and freshly ground pepper
4 strips of bacon, halved

Trim off ends of zucchini. Cut in half lengthwise, scoop out seeds, being careful not to break the shells. Drop zucchini into boiling water to cover. Cover and simmer 8 minutes. Drain and cool. Sauté onions in oil until tender and set aside. Sauté mushrooms until tender and combine with onions, ¼ cup of grated cheese, marjoram, salt, and pepper. Spoon mixture into each shell and sprinkle with remaining cheese. Top with a strip of bacon.

Preheat oven to 350° F. Place stuffed zucchini, side by side, in well-greased shallow baking dish. Bake 15 minutes or until bacon is browned.

ZUCCHINI AND TOMATOES

MAKES 8 SERVINGS   6.1 GRAMS PER SERVING

½ cup chopped onions
2 tablespoons butter or
   margarine
6 cups unpeeled sliced
   zucchini

2½ cups peeled chopped
   tomatoes, fresh or canned
1 teaspoon oregano
1 teaspoon ground ginger
1 teaspoon salt
Freshly ground pepper

Sauté onions in butter until tender. Stir in remaining ingredients. Bring to a boil, cover and simmer slowly 10 minutes or until zucchini is tender but not mushy.

Salads

It comes as a stunning surprise to most people to learn that
many salads can be high in carbohydrates. Take that traditional
restaurant "diet-lunch" salad—jello and lots of citrus fruits
with yogurt. It's loaded with carbohydrate! Or another salad
that looks deceptively safe in carbohydrates but is slathered
with commercial dressing. The commercial dressing is a
time-bomb full of carbohydrates! There is, however, a long
list of salad makings to choose from that are low in carbohydrate, and these are what I make my salads from. The greens
include chicory, endive, escarole, watercress, spinach, cabbage,
and all the lettuces.

Among the low carbohydrate salad add-tos are raw mushrooms, green peppers, anchovies, hard-cooked eggs, capers, olives (green or black), radishes, scallions, and any other low carbohydrate vegetable, like carrot curls and sliced cucumbers.

Nor do you have to limit yourself to green vegetable salads. Blueberries, strawberries, and any melon (all low carbohydrate fruits—and many aren't, so beware!) will turn a salad into a luncheon meal and not run up the gram count beyond the limits I work within.

Make your dressing a delicate blend of herbs, seasonings, and flavorful vinegar and oil—and make it yourself so you know what is in it. Try adding sprigs of your favorite herbs or garlic to vinegar and let it marinate a few days before you use it in dressing—delicious! Have you ever tried making your own mayonnaise? It's easy and delicious, and it, too, can be varied.

Even the simplest salads deserve your care. Just because they aren't cooked, don't think they can be brushed aside without proper preparation. Greens should be fresh and without blemish, thoroughly washed under cold water, then shaken or patted dry, then put in the refrigerator to crisp.

The variety of very low carbohydrate salads that follow reflect many regional and international favorites. San Francisco is famous for its crab Louis, Holland for its wilted spinach salad, Italy for salade Niçoise. You might have fun planning your menu by matching salad and entrée from their country of origin, and decorating the table to enhance the regional theme.

SAMPLE SALAD MENUS

*Avocado-watercress ring**
Casaba melon with cheese

Jellied chicken consommé
*Curried chicken salad**
Daiquiri lime parfait*

Eggs in aspic*
*Crab Louis**
Cantaloupe

Eggs à la Russe*
*Tomato aspic salad**
Persian melon

Egg-drop soup*
*Fruit salad with julienne turkey**
Dessert cheese and espresso

Jellied Madrilène
*Salade Niçoise**
Dessert cheese and espresso

Jellied chicken consommé
*Tomato stuffed with seafood**
Casaba melon

ASPARAGUS VINAIGRETTE
MAKES 8 SERVINGS 5.5 GRAMS PER SERVING

1 cup vinaigrette dressing (see
 Salad Dressings)
4 pounds young cooked
 asparagus spears

Lettuce
4 hard-cooked eggs, quartered
Carrot curls
1 cup mayonnaise (optional)

Pour vinaigrette dressing over hot or cold cooked asparagus and marinate in refrigerator 1 hour or longer. At serving time, carefully drain and arrange asparagus on a bed of lettuce on individual salad plates. Garnish with hard-cooked eggs and crisp carrot curls. Serve with separate bowl of mayonnaise, if desired.

AVOCADO-WATERCRESS RING

MAKES 8 SERVINGS   8.0 GRAMS PER SERVING

1 envelope unflavored gelatin	¾ teaspoon salt
¼ cup fresh lime juice	Cayenne pepper
1 tablespoon chopped onion	1 cup sour cream
1 ½-pound bunch watercress	1 pound peeled cooked shrimp
½ cup boiling water	¼ pound sliced raw mushrooms
1 8-ounce package cream cheese	1 cup fines herbes dressing (see *Salad Dressings*)
3 cups cubed avocado meat	

Combine gelatin, lime juice, onion, watercress stems (reserving leaves for garnish), and water in electric blender. Cover and blend at high speed for 40 seconds. Scrape sides of blender with rubber spatula. Add cream cheese, avocado, salt, and pepper. Cover and blend at high speed. Remove cover while motor is on and slowly add sour cream. Re-cover and blend no more than 30 seconds. Pour avocado mixture into a 6-cup oiled ring mold and chill until set.

Combine shrimp and raw mushrooms with *fines herbes* dressing. Marinate in refrigerator until ready to use. To unmold, dip mold in hot water, wipe mold dry, and immediately invert on large serving platter. Drain shrimp and mushrooms and spoon into center of mold. Surround ring with reserved watercress leaves.

BEET AND ONION SALAD

MAKES 8 SERVINGS   8.4 GRAMS PER SERVING

12 cooked young beets, fresh or canned	1 tablespoon sugar or sugar substitute
1 thinly sliced Bermuda onion	¾ cup red wine vinegar
Salt and freshly ground pepper	Sprigs fresh dill
	4 hard-cooked eggs, quartered

Cut beets with an egg slicer into thin slices and place in a large bowl. Separate Bermuda onion into rings and spread over sliced beets. Sprinkle with salt and pepper. Dissolve sugar in vinegar, pour over beets and carefully toss. Garnish with sprigs of dill and refrigerate 1 hour or longer. Serve in individual bowls or on a bed of lettuce garnished with hard-cooked eggs.

BROCCOLI SALAD

MAKES 8 SERVINGS   5.7 GRAMS PER SERVING

½ cup French dressing (see *Salad Dressings*)
2 pounds cooked fresh broccoli spears
Boston lettuce
⅓ cup mayonnaise
¾ teaspoon fresh lemon juice
Anchovy fillets
4 hard-cooked eggs, quartered

Pour French dressing over hot or cold cooked broccoli and marinate in refrigerator for 1 hour or longer. At serving time, carefully drain and arrange broccoli on a bed of lettuce or individual salad plates. Spoon combination of mayonnaise and lemon juice over broccoli and garnish with anchovy fillets and hard-cooked eggs.

CAESAR SALAD

MAKES 8 SERVINGS   4.1 GRAMS PER SERVING

4 bunches romaine lettuce
2 slices bread
Olive oil
1 garlic clove, halved
1 teaspoon salt
1 teaspoon dry mustard
1 tablespoon fresh lemon juice
¼ teaspoon Worcestershire sauce
1 teaspoon red wine vinegar
2 drops Tabasco sauce
4 tablespoons olive or vegetable oil
1 egg, boiled for 30 seconds only
2 tablespoons grated Parmesan cheese
1 can anchovy fillets, drained and halved
Freshly ground pepper

Thoroughly wash lettuce and tear into bite-size pieces. Dry well and refrigerate 1 hour or longer. Toast bread slices in olive oil until golden brown. Rub both sides of toast with a garlic clove. Remove crusts and cut into small croutons. Sprinkle bottom of salad bowl with salt and rub bowl with a garlic clove. Stir in mustard, lemon juice, Worcestershire sauce, vinegar, and Tabasco until the salt dissolves. Add oil and beat until thoroughly blended. Add lettuce to salad bowl and toss until leaves are evenly coated with dressing. Break egg over salad and toss. Sprinkle with cheese, add anchovies and croutons and toss again. Sprinkle with freshly ground pepper and serve.

CÉLERI RÉMOULADE
MAKES 8 SERVINGS   5.9 GRAMS PER SERVING

4 large celery roots
1½ teaspoons salt
1½ teaspoons fresh lemon juice
4 tablespoons prepared hot mustard (Dijon or Düsseldorf)
3 tablespoons boiling water
⅓ cup olive or vegetable oil
2 tablespoons white wine vinegar
Salt and freshly ground pepper
1 tablespoon chopped fresh parsley

Peel celery roots and cut into thinnest possible slices and into very thin julienne strips about 1 inch long. Toss julienne strips with salt and lemon juice and refrigerate 30 minutes. Rinse in water and dry thoroughly. Add mustard to a warmed mixing bowl and gradually beat in boiling water. Gradually beat in oil and then vinegar to make a thick creamy sauce. Stir in salt and pepper. Combine celery root strips with sauce and refrigerate 3 hours or overnight. Serve as salad or appetizer mounded on bed of lettuce or in individual salad bowls. Sprinkle with parsley.

CURRIED CHICKEN SALAD

MAKES 8 SERVINGS   2.4 GRAMS PER SERVING

3 small onions, peeled and
halved
3 3-pound frying chickens
1 cup diced celery
1 cup small cucumber balls
Salt and freshly ground pepper

½ cup French dressing (see
Salad Dressings)
½ cup mayonnaise
1 teaspoon curry powder
¼ teaspoon soy sauce
Stuffed olives
Radish rosettes

Preheat oven to 350° F.

Place an onion in cavity of each chicken and roast 1 hour
and 15 minutes or until juice runs clear when thigh is pricked.
Discard skin and dice all white meat and choice dark meat for
salad. Combine chicken meat, celery, cucumber balls, salt,
and pepper with French dressing. Refrigerate 1 hour and
drain. Combine mayonnaise, curry, and soy sauce and stir
into chicken mixture. Serve piled on a bed of lettuce or as
filling for large tomatoes or avocados. Garnish with olives and
radishes.

COLE SLAW

MAKES 8 SERVINGS   4.7 GRAMS PER SERVING

⅔ cup mayonnaise
¼ teaspoon prepared hot
mustard
2 teaspoons tomato catsup
1 teaspoon fresh lemon juice
or vinegar
1 teaspoon sugar or sugar
substitute

4 cups shredded cabbage
½ cup grated peeled carrots
(optional)
1 cup minced celery (optional)
½ teaspoon grated onion
(optional)
Salt
1 teaspoon caraway or
celery seeds (optional)

Combine mayonnaise, mustard, catsup, lemon juice, and sugar. Stir into the vegetables and sprinkle with salt. Stir in caraway or celery seeds, if desired. Chill and serve in individual salad bowls.

CRAB LOUIS

MAKES 8 SERVINGS 7.0 GRAMS PER SERVING

1½ cups mayonnaise
⅓ cup heavy cream
¼ cup chili sauce
¼ cup minced green peppers
¼ cup minced scallions, including greens
1 teaspoon prepared horse-radish
1½ teaspoons Worcestershire sauce

Salt and freshly ground pepper
1 head iceberg lettuce, washed and dried
4 cups cooked crab meat, shelled and flaked
4 hard-cooked eggs, quartered
16 cherry tomatoes
8 green olives
2½ tablespoons capers, drained

Blend mayonnaise, cream, chili sauce, green peppers, scallions, horseradish, and Worcestershire in electric blender at low speed for 10 seconds. Scrape sides of blender, add salt and pepper and blend again for 5 seconds. Chill 1 hour or longer. Arrange a bed of lettuce topped by shredded lettuce leaves on individual serving plates. Mound portions of crab meat on top and spoon dressing liberally over crab meat. Serve garnished with hard-cooked eggs, tomatoes, and olives and sprinkle with capers.

CUCUMBER AND ONION SALAD
MAKES 8 SERVINGS 3.6 GRAMS PER SERVING

Salt
1 garlic clove, halved
1 large Bermuda onion, thinly
   sliced
2 large cucumbers, peeled
   and thinly sliced

1 dozen red radishes, thinly
   sliced
1¼ cups sour cream dressing I
   (see *Salad Dressings*)
Salad greens

Lightly sprinkle a wooden salad bowl with salt and rub with garlic. Line bowl with layers of onion, cucumber, and red radish slices. Add sour cream dressing and toss lightly. Chill. Serve on a bed of salad greens or in individual salad bowls.

FRUIT SALAD WITH JULIENNE TURKEY
MAKES 8 SERVINGS 8.2 GRAMS PER SERVING

Salad greens
1 pound cooked turkey breast,
   cut in julienne strips
1 large ripe pineapple, peeled
   and cubed

1 cup blueberries, hulled
1 cup watermelon balls
1 cup lime-mint dressing (see
   Salad Dressings)

Arrange bite-size pieces of salad greens topped with julienne turkey and pineapple in a large salad bowl. Sprinkle salad with blueberries and watermelon balls. Serve salad dressing separately.

GREEK SALAD
MAKES 8 SERVINGS   5.1 GRAMS PER SERVING

Coarse salt
1 garlic clove, halved
4 cups salad greens (lettuce,
   escarole, romaine, chicory)
1 large cucumber, thinly sliced
1 green pepper, seeded and
   sliced into rings
16 cherry tomatoes, halved

¼ cup diced scallions including
   greens
8 radish flowerettes
1 cup cubed feta cheese
¾ cup French dressing (see
   Salad Dressings)
2 dozen black Greek olives
8 anchovy fillets, drained
Chopped fresh mint

Lightly sprinkle a large wooden bowl with salt and rub with cut garlic. Tear salad greens into bite-size pieces and add cucumber, green pepper, tomatoes, and scallions and toss gently. Add radishes and cheese cubes, cover and chill thoroughly. At serving time, sprinkle with French dressing and garnish with olives and rolled anchovy fillets secured with toothpicks. Sprinkle with fresh mint and serve.

HEARTS OF PALM SALAD
MAKES 8 SERVINGS   3.0 GRAMS PER SERVING

1 head Bibb or Limestone
   lettuce
2 pounds cooked asparagus
   spears
2 cups sliced hearts of palm,
   ½ inch thick

¼ cup diced scallions including
   greens
Pimiento strips
Fines herbes dressing (see
   Salad Dressings)

Wash and dry lettuce thoroughly and place on individual salad plates. Arrange asparagus spears, side by side, on top of lettuce. Add sliced hearts of palm and sprinkle with scallions. Garnish with strips of pimiento and serve dressing separately.

SLICED MUSHROOM SALAD

MAKES 8 SERVINGS   2.5 GRAMS PER SERVING

16 large white mushrooms
3 tablespoons fresh lemon
   juice
6 tablespoons olive oil

3 tablespoons chopped fresh
   parsley
Salt and freshly ground pepper

Carefully wipe and trim mushrooms. Slice through caps and stems into very thin slices. Sprinkle with lemon juice. Combine oil, parsley, salt, and pepper and pour over mushrooms. Toss and chill. Serve symmetrically arranged on individual salad plates.

SALADE NIÇOISE

MAKES 8 SERVINGS   8.5 GRAMS PER SERVING

2 cups cold cooked green beans
1 cup sliced cooked beets
1 cup thinly sliced celery
½ cup thinly sliced radishes
2 medium-sized peeled
   tomatoes, cut in wedges
1 cup thinly sliced sweet green
   pepper rings
1 cup thinly sliced red onion
   rings
1 can tuna fish, drained and
   flaked

16 pitted black olives
1 2-ounce can anchovy fillets,
   drained
2 tablespoons olive oil
2 teaspoons prepared hot mustard (Dijon or Düsseldorf)
1 teaspoon chopped fresh or
   ½ teaspoon dried thyme
1 cup French dressing (see
   Salad Dressings)
6 hard-cooked eggs, quartered

Make symmetrical pattern of green beans, beets, celery, radishes, and tomato wedges in a large salad bowl. Surround with an edge of green pepper and onion rings. Sprinkle tuna and olives on top of vegetables. Cut all but 4 anchovy fillets into squares and sprinkle them over salad. Cover and chill.

Moisten 4 anchovy fillets with olive oil and grind with a mortar and pestle into a paste (*pissala*). Pour into a small serving pitcher and chill. Add mustard and thyme to French dressing and chill. At the table, lace the *pissala* over salad and gently toss with French dressing. Heap vegetables onto individual salad plates and garnish with hard-cooked egg wedges.

TOMATO ASPIC SALAD

MAKES 8 SERVINGS   6.4 GRAMS PER SERVING

2 envelopes unflavored gelatin
1 tablespoon fresh lemon juice
1 teaspoon chopped onion
1/2 cup hot chicken broth
2 drops Tabasco
1 tablespoon Worcestershire sauce
1/2 teaspoon celery salt
2 cups V-8 juice
1 heaping cup crushed ice
2 cups tiny cooked bay shrimp
1/2 cup diced, peeled carrots
1/2 cup diced celery
1/4 cup diced scallions, including greens
1/4 cup diced red radishes
1/4 cup diced stuffed green olives
1/4 cup diced sweet gherkin pickles
Mayonnaise or Green Goddess dressing (see *Salad Dressings*)

Combine gelatin, lemon juice, chopped onion, and hot chicken broth in electric blender. Cover and blend at high speed for 40 seconds. Scrape sides of blender with rubber spatula. Add Tabasco, Worcestershire sauce, celery salt, V-8 juice, and crushed ice. Cover and blend again 30 seconds. Pour equal portions of aspic into eight 1-cup molds rinsed in cold water. Chill 10 minutes. Combine shrimp and diced vegetables and toss. Add equal portions of shrimp-vegetable mixture to fill molds. Chill thoroughly until firm. To unmold, dip mold in hot water and immediately invert on a bed of lettuce. Serve mayonnaise or Green Goddess dressing separately.

TOMATOES STUFFED WITH SEAFOOD
MAKES 8 SERVINGS   6.3 GRAMS PER SERVING

½ pound cooked lobster meat
¾ pound cooked crab meat
1 pound cooked shrimp, peeled and deveined
¼ cup French dressing (see Salad Dressings)

¼ teaspoon chopped fresh tarragon or dill
4 large ripe beef steak tomatoes, peeled and halved
1 cup sour cream dressing II (see Salad Dressings)

Cut seafood into bite-size pieces, reserving eight whole shrimps. Stir in French dressing and tarragon so seafood is well coated. Refrigerate for 2 hours. Drain and discard French dressing. Scoop out tomatoes and invert to drain 15 minutes. At serving time, fill tomatoes with a mound of seafood mixture and spoon a generous amount of sour cream dressing over seafood. Crown each with a whole shrimp and serve on lettuce.

WILTED SPINACH SALAD
MAKES 8 SERVINGS   3.1 GRAMS PER SERVING

1 pound fresh young spinach
6 slices crisp bacon, crumbled
4 hard-cooked eggs, chopped
2 tablespoons minced onions
1½ teaspoons salt
½ teaspoon freshly ground pepper

3 tablespoons olive or vegetable oil
1½ tablespoons wine vinegar
½ teaspoon fresh lemon juice
2 tablespoons chicken broth
¼ teaspoon curry powder

Carefully wash and drain spinach. Remove stems and thoroughly dry leaves. Toss spinach leaves with bacon, eggs, onions, salt, and pepper. Cover and chill. Immediately before serving, heat oil, vinegar, lemon juice, broth, and curry. Beat and pour over salad. Toss and serve.

Salad Dressings

FRENCH DRESSINGS

FRENCH DRESSING
MAKES 2 CUPS   .2 GRAM PER TABLESPOON

1½ cups olive or salad oil
 ½ cup wine vinegar or fresh
    lemon juice
  1 teaspoon salt
 ⅛ teaspoon freshly ground
    pepper

⅛ teaspoon dry mustard
   (optional)
1 garlic clove, halved
   (optional)

Combine all ingredients and blend thoroughly until salt dissolves. Chill. Discard garlic before serving.

FINES HERBES DRESSING
MAKES 1¼ CUPS   .2 GRAM PER TABLESPOON

1 cup French dressing
2 tablespoons minced fresh
  parsley
⅛ teaspoon crushed dried basil,
  rosemary, or chervil

⅛ teaspoon crushed dried
   marjoram, tarragon, or
   oregano
1 garlic clove, halved

Combine all ingredients and blend thoroughly. Chill. Discard garlic before serving.

169

LIME-MINT DRESSING
MAKES 1 CUP   .3 GRAM PER TABLESPOON

¾ cup olive or corn oil
¼ cup fresh lime juice
1 teaspoon minced fresh
   parsley
1 teaspoon minced fresh mint

¼ teaspoon dry mustard
½ teaspoon salt
⅛ teaspoon freshly ground
   white pepper

Combine all ingredients and blend thoroughly until salt dissolves. Chill before serving.

ROQUEFORT DRESSING
MAKES 1¼ CUPS   .2 GRAM PER SERVING

1 cup French dressing
¼ cup crumbled Roquefort or
   bleu cheese

Worcestershire sauce (optional)

Blend all ingredients in electric blender at high speed until smooth.

VINAIGRETTE DRESSING
MAKES 1 CUP   .3 GRAM PER TABLESPOON

1 cup French dressing
1½ teaspoons minced sweet
   gherkin pickles
1½ teaspoons drained chopped
   capers

1½ teaspoons minced fresh
   parsley
1½ teaspoons minced chives

Combine all ingredients and blend thoroughly. Chill before serving.

MAYONNAISE BASE DRESSINGS

MAYONNAISE
MAKES 2 CUPS   .1 GRAM PER TABLESPOON

2 egg yolks
2 tablespoons fresh lemon
  juice
2 tablespoons wine vinegar
1 teaspoon dry mustard

½ teaspoon salt
Cayenne pepper
1 cup corn oil
½ cup olive oil

Combine egg yolks, lemon juice, vinegar, mustard, salt, cayenne pepper, and ¼ cup of corn oil in electric blender. Combine remaining corn oil with olive oil. Cover blender and blend at low speed. Immediately remove cover and pour in oils in a slow steady stream. Turn motor off immediately. Chill before serving.

GREEN GODDESS DRESSING
MAKES 2 CUPS   .3 GRAM PER TABLESPOON

1 cup mayonnaise
1 tablespoon fresh lemon juice
1 tablespoon tarragon wine
  vinegar
2 anchovy filets
½ teaspoon chopped garlic

3 tablespoons chopped chives
¼ cup chopped fresh parsley
½ teaspoon salt
Freshly ground pepper
½ cup sour cream

Blend all ingredients (except sour cream) in electric blender at high speed for 10 seconds or until smooth. Occasionally scrape sides of blender with rubber spatula. Fold in sour cream. Chill before serving.

SWEET AND SOUR DRESSING

MAKES 1½ CUPS   .3 GRAM PER TABLESPOON

1 cup mayonnaise
2 tablespoons fresh lemon
   juice
¼ cup water

½ teaspoon honey
2 tablespoons heavy cream
Salt and freshly ground white
   pepper

Blend all ingredients until smooth. Chill before serving.

THOUSAND ISLAND DRESSING

MAKES 1¾ CUPS   .4 GRAM PER TABLESPOON

1 cup mayonnaise
½ cup heavy cream
2 tablespoons chili sauce
1 tablespoon chopped olives
   stuffed with pimiento

1 tablespoon chopped green
   pepper
1 teaspoon chopped onions
1 teaspoon chopped chives

Blend all ingredients in electric blender at high speed for 10 seconds. Occasionally scrape sides of blender with rubber spatula. Chill before serving.

SOUR CREAM DRESSINGS

SOUR CREAM DRESSING I

MAKES 1¼ CUPS   .5 GRAM PER TABLESPOON

1 cup sour cream
1 tablespoon tarragon wine
  vingear
1 tablespoon chopped chives

⅛ teaspoon sugar or sugar
  substitute
¼ teaspoon dry mustard
Salt and cayenne pepper

Combine all ingredients and chill before serving.

SOUR CREAM DRESSING II

MAKES 1 CUP   .3 GRAM PER TABLESPOON

½ cup mayonnaise
½ cup sour cream
1 tablespoon chopped chives

1 teaspoon Worcestershire
  sauce

Combine all ingredients and chill before serving.

Breads

Incredible as it may seem—and it *is*—very low carbohydrate
eaters don't have to forgo bread with their meals any more.
A revolution has taken place, and a new dimension added to
breadmaking with the introduction of very low carbohydrate
bread. This tasteful, deliciously filling bread employs cream
of tartar as the leavening agent and soya powder, a high
protein nutrient, instead of flour. It needs no kneading nor a
long wait for the yeast to make the dough rise. Even if you
are an inexperienced cook, you can—within minutes, by using
your electric blender—make a variety of aromatic, tender
breads with this new method.

Muffins are especially easy to make and keep warm until

serving time. They can be made in advance, frozen, and then warmed up in a bun warmer or the oven to be presented proudly to your guests.

Scones, traditionally served at tea time in England, are also superb at breakfast time as are orange muffins. Almond and sesame wafers are a splendid addition as a snack or at tea time.

Yorkshire pudding, another British dish, originally was cooked in the pan with roast beef so that the drippings would fall upon it giving it its distinctive flavor. But the extravagant drippings are no longer available now that you cook your roast in a slow oven, so try this delicious very low carbohydrate alternative.

Gnocchi alla Florentine, dumplings of Italian origin, is a delectable side dish to a roast or cutlet that can be prepared in advance, refrigerated, or even frozen.

BASIC VERY LOW CARBOHYDRATE BREAD
MAKES 16 SLICES .3 GRAM PER SLICE

3 egg yolks	3 egg whites
3 tablespoons cottage cheese	¼ teaspoon cream of tartar
3 tablespoons soya powder, sifted	Few grains of salt

Preheat oven to 350° F. and lightly butter a small (8-by-4½-inch) Teflon-coated bread pan. Cover and blend egg yolks and cottage cheese in electric blender at medium speed for 10 seconds. Scrape down sides of blender with rubber spatula. Add sifted soya powder, cover, and blend 10 seconds. Scrape down sides of blender again and blend at high speed for 20 seconds or until completely blended. Beat egg whites, cream of tartar, and salt until stiff and peaks form. Carefully fold in half of egg yolk–cheese mixture with rubber spatula so as not to break down stiff egg whites. Carefully fold in remaining egg yolk–cheese mixture.

Pour batter into bread pan and carefully smooth it to edges of pan. Bake 30 minutes at 350° F., lower heat to 300° F., and bake 30 minutes longer or until golden brown and bread pulls away from sides of pan. Cool, slice, and serve.

BREAD CRUMBS
MAKES 2 CUPS .1 GRAM PER TABLESPOON

Prepare Basic Very Low Carbohydrate Bread recipe. Preheat oven to 300° F. Onto a few large Teflon-coated cookie sheets, spoon batter (using a tablespoon) so that spoonsful barely touch. Bake 30 minutes or until light brown. Batter will run together. Cool and crumble into crumbs. Store in a covered container until ready to use.

CHEESE MUFFINS
MAKES 12 MUFFINS .3 GRAM PER MUFFIN

3 egg yolks	3 tablespoons soya powder,
2 tablespoons grated sharp	sifted
Cheddar cheese	3 egg whites
1 tablespoon freshly grated	¼ teaspoon cream of tartar
Parmesan cheese	Few grains of salt
2 teaspoons water	

Preheat oven to 350° F. and lightly butter Teflon-coated muffin pans. Cover and blend egg yolks, cheeses, and water in electric blender at medium speed for 10 seconds. Scrape down sides of blender with rubber spatula. Add sifted soya powder, cover, and blend 10 seconds. Scrape down sides of blender again and blend at high speed for 20 seconds or until completely blended. Beat egg whites, cream of tartar, and salt until stiff and peaks form.

Carefully fold in half of egg yolk–cheese mixture with rubber spatula so as not to break down stiff egg whites. Carefully fold in remaining egg yolk–cheese mixture. Half fill muffin pans with batter. Bake 45 minutes at 350° F. or until golden brown and muffins pull away from sides of pan. Serve piping hot.

ONION MUFFINS
MAKES 12 MUFFINS .6 GRAM PER MUFFIN

3 tablespoons minced onions	3 tablespoons soya powder,
1 tablespoon butter or	sifted
vegetable oil	3 egg whites
3 egg yolks	¼ teaspoon cream of tartar
3 tablespoons cottage cheese	Few grains of salt

Preheat oven to 350° F. and lightly butter Teflon-coated muffin pans. Sauté onions in butter until tender. Drain well on paper towels and set aside. Cover and blend egg yolks and cheese in electric blender at medium speed for 10 seconds. Scrape down sides of blender with rubber spatula. Add sifted soya powder, cover and blend 10 seconds. Scrape down sides of blender again and blend at high speed for 20 seconds or until completely blended. Stir in sautéed onions. Beat egg whites, cream of tartar, and salt until stiff and peaks form.

Carefully fold in half of egg yolk–cheese mixture with rubber spatula so as not to break down stiff egg whites. Carefully fold in remaining egg yolk–cheese mixture. Half fill muffin pans with batter. Bake 45 minutes at 350° F. or until golden brown and muffins pull away from sides of pan. Serve piping hot.

ORANGE MUFFINS

MAKES 12 MUFFINS .4 GRAM PER MUFFIN

3 egg yolks	3 egg whites
3 tablespoons cottage cheese	¼ teaspoon cream of tartar
2 teaspoons grated orange rind	Few grains of salt
3 tablespoons soya powder, sifted	

Preheat oven to 350° F. and lightly butter Teflon-coated muffin pans. Cover and blend egg yolks and cheese in electric blender at medium speed for 10 seconds. Scrape down sides of blender with rubber spatula. Add grated orange rind and sifted soya powder, cover, and blend 10 seconds. Scrape down sides of blender again and blend at high speed for 20 seconds or until completely blended. Beat egg whites, cream of tartar, and salt until stiff and peaks form.

Carefully fold in half of egg yolk–cheese mixture with rubber spatula so as not to break down stiff egg whites. Carefully fold in remaining egg yolk–cheese mixture. Half fill muffin pans with batter. Bake 45 minutes at 350° F. or until golden brown and muffins pull away from sides of pan. Serve piping hot.

POPPY SEED MUFFINS

MAKES 12 MUFFINS .7 GRAM PER MUFFIN

3 egg yolks	3 egg whites
3 tablespoons cottage cheese	¼ teaspoon cream of tartar
3 tablespoons soya powder, sifted	Few grains of salt
	2 teaspoons poppy seeds

Preheat oven to 350° F. and lightly butter Teflon-coated muffin pans. Cover and blend egg yolks and cottage cheese in electric blender at medium speed for 10 seconds. Scrape down sides of blender with rubber spatula. Add sifted soya powder, cover, and blend 10 seconds. Scrape down sides of blender again and blend at high speed for 20 seconds or until completely blended. Beat egg whites, cream of tartar, and salt until stiff and peaks form.

Carefully fold in half of egg yolk–cheese mixture with rubber spatula so as not to break down stiff egg whites. Carefully fold in remaining egg yolk–cheese mixture. Half fill muffin pans with batter and sprinkle with poppy seeds (caraway seeds can be substituted). Bake 45 minutes at 350° F. or until golden brown and muffins pull away from sides of pan. Serve piping hot.

SCONES

MAKES 12 SCONES .9 GRAM PER SCONE

3 eggs
3 tablespoons cottage cheese
1 teaspoon sugar
3 tablespoons soya powder, sifted

⅓ cup heavy cream
¼ teaspoon cream of tartar
Coarse salt (optional)

Preheat oven to 350° F. and lightly butter Teflon-coated muffin pans. Cover and blend eggs, cottage cheese, and sugar in electric blender at medium speed for 10 seconds. Scrape down sides of blender with rubber spatula. Add sifted soya powder, cover, and blend 10 seconds. Scrape down sides of blender again and blend at high speed for 20 seconds or until completely blended. Beat heavy cream and cream of tartar until stiff and peaks form.

Carefully fold in half of egg-cheese mixture with rubber spatula so as not to break down whipped cream. Carefully fold in remaining egg-cheese mixture. Half fill muffin pans with batter. Sprinkle with few grains of coarse salt, if desired. Bake 45 minutes at 350° F. or until golden brown and scones pull away from sides of pan. Serve piping hot.

ALMOND WAFERS
MAKES 36 WAFERS .3 GRAM PER WAFER

3 eggs
3 tablespoons cottage cheese
½ teaspoon sugar or sugar
  substitute
¼ teaspoon almond extract

3 tablespoons soya powder,
  sifted
⅓ cup heavy cream
¼ teaspoon cream of tartar
2 tablespoons slivered
  blanched almonds

Preheat the oven to 300° F. Cover and blend eggs, cottage cheese, sugar, and almond extract in electric blender at medium speed for 10 seconds. Scrape down sides of blender with rubber spatula. Add sifted soya powder, cover, and blend 10 seconds. Scrape down sides of blender again and blend at high speed for 20 seconds or until completely blended. Beat heavy cream and cream of tartar until stiff and peaks form.

Carefully fold in half of egg-cheese mixture with rubber spatula so as not to break down whipped cream. Carefully fold in remaining egg-cheese mixture. On a few large Teflon-coated cookie sheets, spoon 1 tablespoon of batter 1 inch apart. Arrange three or four almond slivers on each wafer. Bake 30 minutes or until light brown. Cool and serve as a snack or at tea time or with fresh strawberries.

SESAME WAFERS
MAKES 36 WAFERS .3 GRAM PER WAFER

4 teaspoons sesame seeds
3 eggs
3 tablespoons cottage cheese
½ teaspoon sugar or sugar
  substitute

3 tablespoons soya powder,
  sifted
⅓ cup heavy cream
¼ teaspoon cream of tartar

Preheat oven to 350° F. and lightly toast sesame seeds for 15 minutes on a Teflon-coated cookie sheet, stirring frequently. Cover and blend eggs, cottage cheese, and sugar in electric blender at medium speed for 10 seconds. Scrape down sides of blender with rubber spatula. Add sifted soya powder, cover, and blend 10 seconds. Scrape down sides of blender again and blend at high speed for 20 seconds or until completely blended. Beat heavy cream and cream of tartar until stiff and peaks form.

Carefully fold in half of egg-cheese mixture with rubber spatula so as not to break down whipped cream. Carefully fold in remaining egg-cheese mixture. On a few large Teflon-coated cookie sheets, spoon 1 tablespoon of batter 1 inch apart. Sprinkle each wafer with toasted sesame seeds. Lower heat of the oven to 300° F. and bake 30 minutes or until light brown. Cool and serve as a snack or as a dipper.

YORKSHIRE PUDDING

MAKES 8 SERVINGS   1.5 GRAMS PER SERVING

4 teaspoons melted butter or margarine	6 tablespoons soya powder, sifted
¼ teaspoon Bovril (beef extract)	½ cup heavy cream
6 eggs	½ teaspoon cream of tartar
6 tablespoons cottage cheese	

Pour melted butter mixed with Bovril into Teflon-coated muffin pans (with sixteen cups) or an 8-by-8-inch ovenproof serving dish. Place pans in oven while it is being preheated to 300° F. Cover and blend eggs and cheese in electric blender at medium speed for 10 seconds. Scrape down sides of blender with rubber spatula. Add sifted soya powder, cover, and blend 10 seconds. Scrape down sides of blender again and blend at high speed for 20 seconds or until completely blended. Beat heavy cream and cream of tartar until stiff and peaks form.

Carefully fold in half of egg-cheese mixture with rubber spatula so as not to break down whipped cream. Carefully fold in remaining egg-cheese mixture. Half fill preheated muffin pans with batter or spoon batter into preheated serving dish. Bake pudding in muffin pans for 45 minutes or in serving dish for 1 hour at 300° F. or until golden brown and pudding pulls away from sides of pan. Serve piping hot.

GNOCCHI ALLA FLORENTINE
MAKES 8 SERVINGS   3.6 GRAMS PER SERVING

1 pound fresh young spinach	Salt and freshly ground white
1 pound ricotta cheese	pepper
1 cup finely grated imported	¼ cup melted butter or
Parmesan cheese	margarine
1 egg, well beaten	¼ cup coarsely grated imported
⅛ teaspoon freshly grated	Parmesan cheese
nutmeg	

Carefully wash and remove stems from spinach, saving only perfect leaves. Tear each leaf into bite-size pieces. Cover and cook spinach over high heat until steam appears. Reduce heat and simmer over very low heat for 5 minutes. Thoroughly drain and press out as much liquid as possible. Mix ricotta cheese, ¾ cup of Parmesan cheese, egg, nutmeg, salt, and pepper. Add cooked spinach and blend well. Shape mixture into 1-inch balls and roll each in remaining finely grated Parmesan cheese. Refrigerate until chilled.

Slip several gnocchi at a time into simmering (not boiling) water in a large skillet. Within a minute, when they float to surface, carefully transfer them with a slotted spoon to buttered shallow ovenproof dish.   Pour some melted butter over all gnocchi and sprinkle each dumpling with coarsely grated Parmesan cheese. Keep warm until ready to serve.

Desserts and Dessert Sauces

Dessert—that grand finale of any meal—seems hopelessly far away to most low carbohydrate gram counters. But it doesn't have to be that way. A wonderful array of colorful, filling low carbohydrate desserts is just a page away.

You can't, of course, serve a hot apple pie with cheese (as the crust is almost pure carbohydrate), but try tart green apple cubes dipped in a cheese fondue or any of the rich, luscious custard, gelatin-based or fruit desserts that follow.

You will also find listed here suggestions for serving a variety of dessert cheeses and fresh fruits—or try one of my very low carbohydrate dessert sauces on fresh peaches, apricots, strawberries, red raspberries, blueberries, or melon balls in combination with one another.

Desserts can be prepared in advance, a great advantage when time is a problem (when is it never?), and they are relatively inexpensive to serve.

DESSERTS

DESSERT CHEESES

A 1-ounce serving of any of these cheeses, served at room temperature, will be .6 gram of carbohydrates or under.

Appenzeller	Feta
Bel Paese	Gruyère
Bonbel	Königskäse
Bleu	Liederkranz
Brie	Petit Suisse
Brillat-Savarin	Pont-l'Evêque
Camembert	Port du Salut
Chantelle	Provolone
Cheddar	Reblochon
Crèma Danica	Roquefort
Creme Chantilly	Samsø
Crème de Gruyère	Stilton
Danish Crème Special	Taleggio
Edam	Vacherin
Esrom	Wensleydale

FRESH FRUIT

Here is a list of fresh fruits that are low (under 10 grams) in carbohydrates for each ½-cup serving, except where indicated (*), or for a quarter section of melons.

Apples (peeled and sliced or cubed)
Apricots (peeled)
Blackberries
Blueberries
Cherries (whole)
Grapefruit (white) sections
Grapes —American type (slip skin)
        —European type and Thompson seedless*

Melons —cantaloupe
        —casaba
        —honeydew
        —Persian
Peaches (peeled and sliced)
Pears (peeled and sliced)
Pineapple (cubed)
Red raspberries
Strawberries
Tangelos (peeled and sectioned)
Watermelon balls

* ⅓ cup serving versus ½ cup

BLANCMANGE WITH RASPBERRIES
MAKES 8 SERVINGS 9.8 GRAMS PER SERVING

1 envelope unflavored gelatin
½ cup boiling water
2½ cups heavy cream
¼ teaspoon almond extract
⅛ teaspoon cinnamon

⅓ cup sifted confectioners' sugar
⅛ teaspoon salt
⅓ cup blanched almonds
1 cup crushed red raspberries
Slivered almonds

Combine gelatin and boiling water in electric blender. Cover and blend at high speed for 40 seconds. Turn motor off. Scrape sides of blender with rubber spatula. Add cream, almond extract, cinnamon, sugar, and salt. Cover and blend at high speed for 10 seconds. With motor still on, remove cover and add blanched almonds. Turn motor off immediately. Pour mixture into a saucepan, stir, and simmer over medium heat until thickened. Pour into eight small individual molds, rinsed in cold water. Chill until firm, about 2 hours.

To unmold, dip outside of each mold in hot water and immediately invert onto individual dessert dishes. Pour 3 tablespoons of raspberries over each portion and sprinkle with slivered almonds.

CHEESE FONDUE WITH GREEN APPLES
MAKES 8 SERVINGS   9.6 GRAMS PER SERVING

2 tablespoons butter or margarine
½ teaspoon dry mustard
1 tablespoon flour
½ cup hard cider
½ cup milk

2 cups diced natural sharp Cheddar cheese
Salt and freshly ground white pepper
4 cups peeled, cubed tart green apples

Melt butter in heavy fondue pot and slowly stir in mustard and flour with a wooden spoon. Add cider and stir until mixture thickens. Lower heat and gradually add diced cheese. Stir in a figure-eight motion until all cheese has been added and melted. Season with salt and pepper to taste. At dinner table guests dip bite-size cubes of apples into cheese fondue using fondue forks or long wooden skewers.

COEUR À LA CRÈME
MAKES 8 SERVINGS   8.8 GRAMS PER SERVING

1 pound creamed cottage cheese
1 pound softened cream cheese
2 cups heavy cream
⅛ teaspoon salt

2 tablespoons sifted confectioners' sugar or sugar substitute
2 cups halved fresh strawberries

Blend cottage cheese and cream cheese until smooth. Stir in cream and salt. Spoon mixture to fill individual coeur à la crème ceramic molds lined with dampened cheesecloth. Lightly fold overlapping ends of cheesecloth over top of each portion and stand molds on a cookie sheet to drain overnight in refrigerator.

At serving time, unmold onto chilled dessert plates and carefully remove cheesecloth. Sift sugar over strawberries (or raspberries) and arrange them attractively around each portion.

COFFEE BAVARIAN CREAM
MAKES 8 SERVINGS   9.7 GRAMS PER SERVING

2 envelopes unflavored gelatin	3 egg yolks
1 cup hot strong coffee	2 cups heavy cream
1 ounce German sweet chocolate, chopped	1 tablespoon light rum
	1½ cups crushed ice
4 tablespoons sugar or sugar substitute	⅛ teaspoon vanilla extract

Blend gelatin and hot coffee in electric blender at high speed for 20 seconds. Scrape sides of blender with rubber spatula. Add chocolate and 3 tablespoons of sugar, cover, and blend again for 10 seconds. With motor still running, remove cover and add egg yolks, 1½ cups of cream, rum, and crushed ice. Re-cover and blend for 20 seconds. Pour mixture into eight small individual dessert dishes or sherbet glasses. Chill until firm, about 2 hours. At serving time, whip ½ cup of cream, 1 tablespoon of sugar, and vanilla until stiff and spoon generously onto each portion.

COUPE DE LUXE

MAKES 8 SERVINGS 6.7 GRAMS PER SERVING

1 cup halved fresh straw-
  berries
1 cup peeled, sliced fresh
  peaches

1 cup fresh pineapple cubes
½ cup brandy
1 fifth chilled pink French
  champagne (extra dry)

Stir fruit and brandy together and marinate in refrigerator for 1 hour or longer. Fill large chilled goblets half full of fruit combination. At table, pour champagne over fruit and serve.

DAIQUIRI LIME PARFAIT

MAKES 8 SERVINGS 7.8 GRAMS PER SERVING

¼ cup fresh lime juice
¼ cup cold water
1 envelope unflavored gelatin
4 egg yolks
Dash salt
½ cup sifted confectioners'
  sugar

3 tablespoons light rum
3 to 4 drops of green food
  coloring
¾ cup heavy cream
4 egg whites
½ cup heavy cream, whipped
Fresh mint leaves

Combine lime juice and water and sprinkle with gelatin. Set aside for 5 minutes. Stir egg yolks, salt, and sugar with a wooden spoon over simmering water in top of double boiler until custard thickens and coats the spoon. Cool slightly. Stir in gelatin mixture, rum, food coloring, and cream. Beat egg whites until stiff but not dry and fold gradually into custard. Pour into parfait glasses and refrigerate or freeze for 2 hours until firm. At serving time, garnish with whipped cream and fresh mint leaves.

FROZEN GRAND MARNIER MOUSSE
MAKES 8 SERVINGS   7.2 GRAMS PER SERVING

8 oranges
6 egg yolks
2 tablespoons sugar
1 tablespoon grated orange
   rind
½ cup fresh orange juice,
   strained

2 tablespoons Grand Marnier
2 cups heavy cream, whipped
3 tablespoons shredded fresh
   coconut
Fresh mint leaves

Cut zigzag with a sharp knife around oranges about one-third of the way down from top. Plunge oranges into boiling water and let stand for 5 minutes. Cool slightly and remove top of each orange, scoop out pulp, reserving it for its juice, and freeze orange shells. Beat egg yolks and sugar in top of double boiler over simmering water for 3 minutes. Stir in orange rind. Press orange pulp with back of spoon through a sieve to extract ½ cup of juice. Stir orange juice and Grand Marnier into egg mixture. Place top of double boiler in bowl of crushed ice and beat again for 2 minutes or until thick and creamy. Fold whipped cream into egg mixture and spoon mousse into frozen orange shells, mounding it high. Freeze at least 2 hours. At serving time, sprinkle with coconut and garnish with mint leaves.

PEACHES ROYALE
MAKES 8 SERVINGS   9.5 GRAMS PER SERVING

4 large peeled, fresh peaches,
   halved
1¼ cups fresh strawberries

⅓ cup brandy
2 cups strawberry Chantilly
   sauce (see *Dessert Sauces*)

Arrange peach halves and strawberries in a large serving bowl. Sprinkle brandy over fruit, cover, and refrigerate at least 2 hours. Spoon brandied fruit into individual dessert dishes at the table and serve Chantilly sauce separately.

PETIT POT DE CRÈME
MAKES 8 SERVINGS 9.7 GRAMS PER SERVING

2 cups heavy cream	1 tablespoon grated orange
5 egg yolks	rind
5 tablespoons sugar	2 tablespoons Grand Marnier
1/8 teaspoon salt	8 candy flowers or fresh violets

Heat cream to just below a boil in top of double boiler. Beat egg yolks, sugar, and salt until light and lemon-colored. Gradually stir in the cream. Strain mixture back into double boiler and heat over simmering water. Stir with a wooden spoon until custard thickens and coats spoon. Immediately set pan into iced water to stop the cooking. Stir in orange rind and Grand Marnier and pour into individual crème pots. Chill thoroughly. Garnish with candy flowers or violets.

STRAWBERRIES ROMANOFF
MAKES 8 SERVINGS 8.5 GRAMS PER SERVING

3½ cups fresh strawberries	2 tablespoons brandy
2 tablespoons sifted confec-	1 cup heavy cream
tioners' sugar (if needed)	1 tablespoon kirsch
2 tablespoons Cointreau	

Thoroughly wash and drain strawberries. Remove stem ends. Arrange strawberries in large serving bowl and sprinkle with confectioners' sugar. Pour mixture of Cointreau and brandy over berries, cover and chill for several hours.

At serving time, beat cream and kirsch until stiff. Spoon berries into individual dessert bowls at the table and top with whipped cream.

ZABAGLIONE
MAKES 8 SERVINGS   9.9 GRAMS PER SERVING

12 egg yolks
1 cup Marsala wine

5 tablespoons sugar or sugar
substitute

Beat egg yolks, Marsala, and sugar in top of large double boiler over simmering water until mixture increases 4 times its original volume. Occasionally scrape sides and bottom of pan with rubber spatula. Serve while still hot in sherbet glasses or as a sauce for strawberries or red raspberries.

DESSERT SAUCES

GERVAISE SAUCE

MAKES 1¾ CUPS .4 GRAM PER TABLESPOON

For fresh fruit compotes

2 3-ounce packages cream
  cheese

1 cup sour cream
1 tablespoon brandy

Blend all ingredients until smooth and serve.

RUM CUSTARD SAUCE

MAKES 2 CUPS .8 GRAM PER TABLESPOON

For blueberries, sliced peaches, red raspberries, or strawberries

⅓ cup milk
⅓ cup heavy cream
1-inch piece vanilla bean
  2 egg yolks

1½ tablespoons sugar
  2 tablespoons dark rum
  ½ cup heavy cream, whipped

Heat milk and cream with vanilla bean to just below a boil
in top of double boiler. Discard vanilla bean. Beat egg yolks
and sugar until light and lemon-colored. Gradually stir in milk

195

and cream mixture. Strain mixture back into double boiler and heat over simmering water. Stir with wooden spoon until custard thickens and coats spoon. Immediately set pan into cold water to stop cooking. At serving time, stir rum into custard and fold in whipped cream.

SABAYON SAUCE

MAKES 2 CUPS   .8 GRAM PER TABLESPOON

For sliced peaches, red raspberries, or strawberries

4 egg yolks	¼ teaspoon grated lemon rind
½ cup dry white wine	1 teaspoon fresh lemon juice
2 tablespoons sugar	¼ cup heavy cream, whipped

Beat egg yolks, wine, sugar, lemon rind, and lemon juice in top of double boiler over simmering water until mixture increases four times its original volume. Occasionally scrape sides and bottom of pan with rubber spatula. Place top of double boiler in bowl of crushed ice and continue to beat until chilled. Fold whipped cream into sauce and chill until ready to use.

STRAWBERRY CHANTILLY

MAKES 2 CUPS   .8 GRAM PER TABLESPOON

For peaches royale

¾ cup fresh strawberries, hulled and crushed	3 tablespoons sifted confectioners' sugar or sugar substitute
⅓ cup heavy cream	

Combine crushed strawberries, cream, and confectioners' sugar. Cover and refrigerate along with the beater for 2 hours. At serving time, beat until stiff.

Appendix A

ROASTING MEATS

∿

Meat should be at room temperature before roasting and the oven should be preheated to the specified temperature before placing the meat, fat side up, in the oven.

In a gas or electric oven, insert a meat thermometer in the center of the thickest part of the lean meat away from the bone *before* placing the roast in the oven.

In a microwave oven, the meat thermometer is inserted in the same manner but during the standing time *after* the roast has been removed from the oven. During this time, the internal temperature will rise about 20° Fahrenheit.

All roasts carve more easily with a 5- to 10-minute standing period after removal from the oven. It should be noted that the roast will continue to cook during this period with a corresponding temperature rise so the thermometer should remain in position during this process.

TIMETABLE FOR ROASTING MEATS

Roast	Weight	Preheated oven temperature	Interior temperature*	Approximate roasting time per pound	
				Gas or electric	Microwave
	Pounds	Degrees F.	Degrees F.	Minutes	Minutes
BEEF					
Standing ribs:					
Rare	6–8	300	140	18–20	5½
Medium			160	22–25	6½
Well done			170	27–30	7½
Rolled ribs:					
Rare	5–7	300	140	32	6½
Medium			160	38	7½
Well done			170	48	8½
LAMB					
Leg	5–8	300	175–180	30–35	9
Boned and rolled	3–5	300	175–180	40–45	9½
Shoulder	4–6	300	175–180	30–35	9
PORK—Fresh					
Loin	5–7	350	185	40–45	9½
Fresh ham	10–12	350	185	30–35	9
PORK—Smoked Ham					
Precooked—half	5–7	325	160	10–15	5
—whole	10–12	325	160	15–20	5½
Tenderized—half	5–7	325	160	20–25	6½
—whole	10–12	325	160	25–30	7
Picnic	3–10	300	170	35	7½
VEAL					
Leg roast	5–8	300	170	25–35	8
Loin	4–6	300	170	30–35	9
Rib—rack	3–5	300	170	30–35	9
Shoulder	5–8	300	170	25–35	8
Boned and rolled	4–6	300	170	40–45	9½

* Gas or electric oven—insert thermometer *during* roasting time. Microwave ovens—insert thermometer *after* roast is removed from the oven.

Appendix B

CARBOHYDRATE GRAM COUNTER

	grams
Abalone, 4 oz. cooked	3.9
Almond extract, 1 teaspoon	.1
Almonds, ½ cup slivered or chopped	12.4
Anchovies, canned, 1 oz. drained	.1
Anchovy paste, 1 teaspoon	.3
Apple cider, ½ cup	12.8
fermented, ½ cup	1.2
Applejack, 1 oz.	.1
Apple juice, ½ cup	13.4
Apples, ½ cup peeled and diced	7.4
½ cup unpeeled and sliced	9.5
spiced love, 1 small	3.5
Apricots, fresh, ½ cup peeled and sliced	9.0
dried, 2 halves	5.0
Arrowroot, 1 tablespoon	7.0
Artichoke bottoms, canned, 1 large	5.0
canned, 1 small	2.0
Artichoke hearts	
canned, 3 oz.	5.3
frozen, 3 oz.	4.0
marinated, 3 oz.	6.0

Artichokes, fresh, 1 large cooked	11.2
Asparagus, fresh, 6 stalks cooked	3.0
frozen, 6 stalks cooked	3.9
Avocado, California, 1 cup cubes	9.0
Florida, 1 cup cubes	13.0
Bacon, 1 strip broiled or fried	.2
Bacon drippings	0
Baking powder, cream of tartar, 1 teaspoon	1.0
Bamboo shoots, canned, ½ cup	1.7
Bananas, 1 large	30.2
Bean sprouts, mung, ½ cup cooked	5.9
soy, ½ cup cooked	.9
Beans	
baked, canned, pork and molasses, ½ cup	23.9
canned, pork and tomato sauce, ½ cup	24.8
green, canned, ½ cup cooked	3.6
fresh, cut, ½ cup cooked	3.7
French-style, ½ cup cooked	2.8
raw, ½ cup trimmed	3.8
frozen, cut, ½ cup cooked	6.5
French-style, ½ cup cooked	5.0
kidney, canned, ½ cup drained	19.7
lima, canned, ½ cup cooked	15.9
fresh baby, ½ cup cooked	16.8
frozen baby, ½ cup cooked	19.2
wax, canned, ½ cup cooked	5.9
fresh, ½ cup cooked	3.8
frozen, ½ cup cooked	7.0
Beef	0
Beef bouillon (see Bouillon)	
Beef consommé (see Consommé)	
Beef heart, lean, 4 oz. cooked	.8
Beef kidney, 4 oz. cooked	.9
Beef liver, calves', 4 oz. cooked	4.6
steer, 4 oz. cooked	6.0

Beef tongue, canned, 4 oz. cooked	.8
fresh, 4 oz. cooked	.5
Beet greens, 1 cup trimmed	1.9
Beets, canned, ½ cup	7.2
fresh, ½ cup cooked	5.9
Belgium endive, 1 small	1.8
1 large	5.4
Bitter lemon, 6 oz.	23.4
Blackberries, canned, ½ cup unsweetened	11.0
fresh, ½ cup	8.2
frozen, ½ cup sweetened	27.7
½ cup unsweetened	12.9
Blueberries, canned, ½ cup unsweetened	11.8
fresh, ½ cup	9.0
frozen, ½ cup sweetened	30.2
½ cup unsweetened	15.0
Bologna, 1 oz. slice	1.1
Bouillon, beef, canned, 1 cup diluted	2.8
10½ oz. can undiluted	6.3
cube or powder	.5
chicken, canned, 1 cup diluted	1.9
10½ oz. can undiluted	4.2
cube or powder	.6
Bovril, 1 teaspoon	.5
Boysenberries, canned, ½ cup unsweetened	11.0
fresh, ½ cup	8.2
frozen, ½ cup sweetened	27.7
½ cup unsweetened	12.9
Brains, all kinds, 4 oz.	.9
Brandy	0
Bread crumbs, commercial, 1 tablespoon	4.7
very low carbohydrate, 1 tablespoon	.1
Breads	
cracked wheat, 1 slice	12.0
French, 1 small slice	10.4
gluten, 1 slice	5.6

Italian, 1 small slice	14.5
protein, 1 slice	8.7
raisin, 1 slice	13.3
rye, 1 slice	12.1
very low carbohydrate, 1 slice	.3
white, 1 slice	12.7
whole wheat, 1 slice	11.0
Broccoli, fresh, ½ cup cooked	3.5
½ cup raw flowerettes	5.8
frozen, ½ cup cooked	4.4
Brussels sprouts, fresh, ½ cup cooked	5.8
frozen, ½ cup cooked	7.4
Butter, 1 tablespoon	.1
Cabbage, white, 1 cup shredded	5.4
red, 1 cup shredded	7.0
Savoy, 1 cup shredded	4.4
Calvados, 1 oz.	.1
Calves' liver, 4 oz.	4.6
Cantaloupe, 1 quarter	4.2
Capers, 1 teaspoon	.3
Caraway seeds, 1 teaspoon	2.0
Carrots, canned, ½ cup cooked slices	5.3
fresh, ½ cup cooked slices	5.4
½ cup peeled raw sticks	5.6
frozen, ½ cup cooked slices	7.7
Casaba melon, 1 quarter	3.9
Cashew nuts, ½ cup	20.0
Catsup, 1 tablespoon	4.3
Cauliflower, fresh, ½ cup cooked	2.5
½ cup raw flowerettes	2.2
frozen, ½ cup cooked	3.0
Caviar, 1 oz.	.9
Celeriac, ½ cup peeled	5.0
Celery, ½ cup cooked slices	2.6
½ cup raw strips	2.1

Celery root, ½ cup peeled	5.0
Celery seed, 1 teaspoon	.1
Cereals	
bran flakes, 1 cup	30.0
cornflakes, 1 cup	21.0
sugar frosted, 1 cup	35.0
oatmeal, 1 cup cooked	26.0
Rice Krispies, 1 cup	25.1
Special "K," 1 cup	14.0
wheat flakes, 1 cup	23.0
Champagne, dry American, 4 oz.	3.0
dry French, 4 oz.	1.0
Cheese	
American, 1 oz.	1.0
appenzeller, 1 oz.	.5
Bel Paese, 1 oz.	.6
bonbell, 1 oz.	.6
bondost, 1 oz.	.6
bleu, 1 oz.	1.0
brie, 1 oz.	.6
brillat-Savarin, 1 oz.	.6
camembert, 1 oz.	.5
chantelle, 1 oz.	.6
Cheddar, natural, 1 oz.	.6
processed, 1 oz.	.5
Christian IX, 1 oz.	.6
cottage, creamed, 1 oz.	.8
skimmed milk, 1 oz.	.6
cream, 1 oz.	.7
Crèma Danica, 1 oz.	.6
crème Chantilly, 1 oz.	.6
crème de Gruyère, 1 oz.	.6
Danish crème special, 1 oz.	.6
double Gloucester, 1 oz.	.5
Edam, 1 oz.	.3
esrom, 1 oz.	.6

feta, 1 oz.	.5
fontina, 1 oz.	.6
gorgonzola, 1 oz.	.4
gouda, 1 oz.	.5
Gruyère, 1 oz.	.6
Havarti, 1 oz.	.5
Icelandic banquet, 1 oz.	.5
Jarlsberg, 1 oz.	.6
Königskäse, 1 oz.	.6
La Grappe, 1 oz.	.5
Liederkranz, 1 oz.	.4
manchego, 1 oz.	.6
mozzarella, 1 oz.	.3
muenster, 1 oz.	.6
Parmesan, 1 oz.	.8
1 tablespoon grated	.2
petit Suisse, 1 oz.	.6
Pont-l'Evêque, 1 oz.	.5
Port du Salut, 1 oz.	.3
provolone, 1 oz.	.5
reblochon, 1 oz.	.6
ricotta, 1 oz.	1.0
Romano, 1 oz.	.8
Roquefort, 1 oz.	.5
samso, 1 oz.	.6
stilton, 1 oz.	.6
Swiss, 1 oz.	1.0
taleggio, 1 oz.	.6
Tijuana, 1 oz.	.6
tilsiter, 1 oz.	.6
vacherin, 1 oz.	.5
Wensleydale, 1 oz.	.5
Cherries, canned, ½ cup unsweetened	11.5
½ cup in heavy syrup	29.5
fresh, sour, ½ cup	8.2
sweet, ½ cup	10.0

Chicken	0
Chicken bouillon (*see* Bouillon)	
Chicken broth, 1 cup	.1
Chicken consommé (*see* Consommé)	
Chicken gizzards, 4 oz.	.8
Chicken hearts, 4 oz.	.2
Chicken livers, 4 oz.	3.3
Chili powder, 1 tablespoon	.5
Chili sauce, 1 tablespoon	3.8
Chinese snow peas (*see* Peas)	
Chives, 1 tablespoon chopped	.1
Chocolate, bitter, 1 oz.	7.7
semi-sweet, 1 oz.	18.1
sweet, 1 oz.	15.6
Chocolate fudge syrup, 1 tablespoon	7.6
Chutney, apple, 1 tablespoon	13.1
Cider, apple, ½ cup	12.8
½ cup fermented	1.2
Clam juice, 1 cup	5.0
Clams, canned, 4 oz. drained	2.1
4 oz. with juice	3.2
raw, 4 oz.	1.5
Cloves	0
Club soda, 4 oz.	0
Coca Cola, 6 oz.	18.0
diet, 6 oz.	9.0
Coconut, dried, 1 cup shredded	49.0
fresh, 1 cup shredded	7.6
Coffee, black, 1 cup	.4
espresso, 1 cup	.8
instant black, 1 cup	.7
decaffeinated, 1 cup	.7
freeze dried, 1 cup	.8
Cointreau, 1 oz.	3.9
Consommé, beef, canned, 1 cup diluted	2.6
½ cup undiluted	3.1

chicken, canned, 1 cup diluted	1.9
½ can undiluted	2.1
Madrilène, ½ can undiluted	2.4
Coriander, 1 tablespoon chopped	.2
Corn, canned, ½ cup	18.0
fresh, ½ cup	13.1
frozen, ½ cup	17.1
Corn oil	0
Cornstarch, 1 tablespoon	7.0
Corn syrup, 1 tablespoon	15.0
Crab meat, canned, 4 oz.	1.3
fresh, 4 oz. cooked	.6
frozen, 4 oz. cooked	.6
Crab, soft shelled, 1 small	.2
Cranberries, fresh, ½ cup	6.1
Cranberry juice, ½ cup	20.8
Cranberry sauce, 1 tablespoon	5.3
Cream	
half-and-half, 1 cup	11.0
heavy, 1 cup	7.0
light, 1 cup	10.0
sour, 1 cup	7.7
whipped, 1 cup	3.6
Cream of tartar, baking powder, 1 teaspoon	1.0
Cress, water, 1 cup trimmed	1.9
Cucumber, ½ cup peeled and cubed	2.3
½ cup unpeeled slices	3.2
Cumin seeds, 1 teaspoon	.1
Curaçao, 1 oz.	9.5
Curry powder, 1 teaspoon	1.6
Dandelion greens, 1 cup trimmed	6.9
Dates, 1 date	5.8
Dewberries, canned, ½ cup unsweetened	11.0
fresh, ½ cup	8.2
frozen, ½ cup sweetened	27.7

Dill pickles, 1 tablespoon chopped	.3
Duck	0
Eggplant, ½ cup cooked	4.1
Egg, whites, 1 medium cooked or raw	.2
whole, 1 medium cooked or raw	.3
yolk, 1 medium cooked or raw	.1
Endive, Belgium, 1 small	1.8
1 large	5.4
Escarole, 1 cup trimmed	2.9
Fats	
bacon	0
chicken	0
cooking oil	0
vegetable oil	0
Fennel, ½ cup strips	2.0
Figs	
canned, ½ cup sweetened	19.0
½ cup unsweetened	14.0
Kadota, ½ cup unsweetened	11.1
dried, 1 large	15.0
fresh, 1 large	7.6
Finocchio (see Fennel)	
Fish (see individual names)	0
Flounder	0
Flour	
buckwheat, 1 cup	93.8
cake, 1 cup sifted	78.6
cornmeal, 1 cup	115.5
gluten, 1 cup sifted	64.2
rye, 1 cup sifted	68.6
soybean (powder)	
natural, 1 cup sifted	19.7
low fat, 1 cup sifted	22.7

wheat, all-purpose, 1 cup sifted	88.2
Wondra, 1 cup	86.1
whole wheat, 1 cup	97.2
Frankfurter, 1 cooked	.7
Frogs' legs	0
Fruit (see individual names)	
Garlic, ½ teaspoon minced	.7
¼ teaspoon crushed	.7
Garlic salt, 1 teaspoon	1.0
Gelatin, unflavored	0
fruit flavors, ½ cup sweetened	16.8
unsweetened	0
Ginger, 1 teaspoon ground	.3
Ginger ale, 6 oz.	16.5
diet, 6 oz.	.8
Gingersnaps, 1 small	2.5
Gizzards, chicken, 4 oz. cooked	.8
Goose liver pâté, 1 tablespoon	1.3
Graham cracker crumbs, 1 cup	80.0
Grand Marnier, 1 oz.	3.6
Grape juice, canned, ½ cup sweetened	21.2
½ cup unsweetened	17.4
frozen, ½ cup sweetened	16.6
Grapefruit, canned, ½ cup sweetened	22.8
½ cup unsweetened	9.0
fresh, ½ medium	14.0
Grapefruit juice, canned, ½ cup sweetened	16.0
½ cup unsweetened	12.0
fresh, ½ cup	11.3
frozen, ½ cup sweetened	14.0
½ cup unsweetened	12.0
Grapes, canned, ½ cup with syrup	22.7
fresh, American-type, ½ cup	7.5
European-type, ⅓ cup	9.5
Thompson seedless, ⅓ cup	9.5

Grapevine leaves, 1 pound jar washed and drained	9.2
Green beans (*see* Beans, green)	
Green onions (*see* Scallions)	
Green pepper, 1 medium	3.0
Grenadine syrup, 1 tablespoon	7.6
Haddock	0
Halibut	0
Ham, boiled	0
canned, 1 oz.	.3
deviled, 1 tablespoon	.2
fresh	0
prosciutto	0
smoked	0
Hare (rabbit)	0
Heart, beef, lean, 4 oz. cooked	.8
chicken, 4 oz. cooked	.1
Hearts of palm, 10½ oz. can drained	1.5
Herbs	0
Herring, fresh	0
marinated in cream, 1 small piece	.8
pickled or smoked	0
Honey, 1 tablespoon	17.2
Honeydew melon, 1 quarter	5.5
Horseradish, prepared, 1 teaspoon	.4
Ice cream, vanilla, ¼ pint (1 cup)	15.1
chocolate, ¼ pint	16.6
sherbet with milk, ¼ pint	44.0
with water, ¼ pint	35.2
strawberry, ¼ pint	15.9
Jams and jellies	
apple butter, 1 tablespoon	8.4
apple-mint, 1 tablespoon dietetic	5.4
1 tablespoon sweetened	13.0

apricot, 1 tablespoon	10.0
grape, 1 tablespoon	10.1
orange marmalade, 1 tablespoon	10.9
red currant, 1 tablespoon	10.1
strawberry preserves, 1 tablespoon	10.0
Juices (*see* individual names)	
Kale, fresh, ½ cup cooked	2.2
frozen, ½ cup cooked	3.1
Kidneys	
beef, 4 oz. cooked	.9
calf, 4 oz. cooked	.1
lamb, 4 oz. cooked	1.0
pork, 4 oz. cooked	.8
veal, 4 oz. cooked	.9
Kirsch, 1 oz.	8.8
Lamb	0
Lard	0
Leeks, 1 tablespoon chopped	1.2
soup mix, 1 package	15.3
Lemon juice, 1 tablespoon	1.0
Lemon rind, 1 tablespoon grated	.7
Lentils, ½ cup cooked	19.5
Lettuce	
Bibb, 1 cup trimmed	1.9
Boston, 1 cup trimmed	1.9
iceberg, 1 cup trimmed	1.8
leaf, 1 cup trimmed	1.7
Romaine, 1 cup trimmed	1.7
Lima beans (*see* Beans)	
Lime juice, 1 tablespoon	1.3
Lime rind, 1 tablespoon grated	.7
Liver, beef, 4 oz. cooked	6.0
calf, 4 oz. cooked	4.6
chicken, 4 oz. cooked	3.3

goose, 4 oz. cooked	6.1
lamb, 4 oz. cooked	3.3
pork, 4 oz. cooked	4.2
Liver pâté, 1 tablespoon	.5
Liverwurst, 1 oz.	.5
Lobster, fresh or canned, 4 oz.	.4
Lox	0
Lunch meat, 1 oz. slice	1.1
Macaroni, ½ cup cooked firm	19.5
½ cup cooked tender and rinsed	15.1
Madeira wine, 1 oz.	2.1
Mandarin orange, 10½ oz. can unsweetened	6.1
Maple syrup, 1 tablespoon	13.0
Margarine, 1 tablespoon	.1
Mayonnaise, homemade, 1 tablespoon	.1
real, commercial, 1 tablespoon	.2
salad dressing, commercial, 1 tablespoon	1.8
Melons (*see individual names*)	
Milk	
canned, evaporated, 1 cup unsweetened	24.0
1 cup skimmed	26.4
canned, condensed, 1 cup sweetened	164.8
dry, 1 cup whole	9.8
1 cup nonfat	11.6
fresh, 1 cup whole	12.0
1 cup skimmed	12.5
Molasses, light, 1 tablespoon	13.0
Monosodium glutamate (MSG)	0
Mushrooms, canned, ½ cup drained	2.9
fresh, ½ cup raw or cooked	1.4
Mussels, 4 oz. meat	3.8
Mustard, dry	0
prepared, brown, 1 teaspoon	.5
hot, 1 teaspoon	.4
yellow, 1 teaspoon	.6
Mustard greens, 1 cup trimmed	2.9

Nasturtium leaves, 1 cup trimmed	2.0
Nectarines, ½ cup peeled slices	15.2
Noodles, egg, ½ cup cooked tender and rinsed	17.6
fried, canned, 1 oz.	16.7
Nuts (*see* individual names)	

Oils	0
Okra, ½ cup cooked	5.3
Oleomargine, 1 tablespoon	.1
Olive oil	0
Olives, green, ripe or stuffed, 1 large	.1
Onion(s)	
chopped, 1 cup	15.0
cocktail, 1 tablespoon	.3
cooked, ½ cup	5.8
dehydrated flakes, 1 tablespoon	1.1
grated, 1 tablespoon	1.2
green (scallions), chopped, 1 tablespoon	.6
soup mix, 1 package	15.3
Orange juice	
canned, ½ cup sweetened	15.8
fresh, ½ cup	13.0
frozen, ½ cup unsweetened	13.5
Orange rind, 1 tablespoon grated	.7
Oranges, fresh, ½ cup sections	14.9
Mandarin, 10½ oz. can unsweetened	6.1
Oysters, 4 oz. raw	3.9
Oxtail	0

Palm, hearts of, 10½ oz. can drained	1.5
Pancake syrup, 1 tablespoon	13.5
Parsley, 1 tablespoon chopped	.2
Parsnips, ½ cup cooked	15.8
Partridge	0
Pastrami, 1 oz.	.4

Pâté

de foie gras, 1 tablespoon	1.3
liver, 1 tablespoon	.5

Peaches

canned, ½ cup sweetened	13.2
½ cup unsweetened	9.9
fresh, ½ cup peeled slices	8.0
frozen, ½ cup sweetened	22.3
Peanut butter, 1 tablespoon	2.8
Peanuts, ½ cup halves or chopped	13.0

Pears

canned, ½ cup sweetened	22.5
½ cup unsweetened	19.8
fresh, ½ cup peeled slices	9.4

Peas

canned, ½ cup drained	14.4
fresh and frozen, ½ cup cooked	9.8
snow pea pods, fresh, ½ cup cooked	3.7
frozen, ½ cup cooked	4.5
Pecans, ½ cup halves or chopped	7.6
Pepsi Cola, 6 oz.	19.5
diet, 6 oz.	5.7
Peppers, green, 1 medium	3.0
red, 1 medium	4.0
Tuscan vinegar, 1 small	.2
Pernod, 1 oz.	1.1
Persian melon, 1 quarter	4.5
Persimmons, 1 medium	20.0
Pheasant	0
Pickle relish, 1 tablespoon	3.4

Pickles

chow-chow, sour, 1 oz.	1.2
sweet, 1 oz.	7.7
cucumber, 1 oz.	5.1
dill, 1 oz.	.6
sour, 1 oz.	.6
sweet gherkin, 1 oz.	10.3

Pigs' feet	0
Pimiento, 4 oz. jar drained	4.6
Pine nuts, 1 tablespoon chopped	.7
Pineapple	
canned, ½ cup sweetened	17.1
½ cup unsweetened	11.6
fresh, ½ cup diced	9.5
frozen, ½ cup sweetened	27.3
Pineapple juice, canned, ½ cup unsweetened	17.0
frozen, ½ cup sweetened	16.0
Pistachio nuts, ½ cup shelled	11.8
Pizza pie with cheese, 1 piece	25.2
Plums	
canned, ½ cup sweetened	25.3
½ cup unsweetened	12.6
fresh, 1 medium	7.0
Poppy seed, 1 teaspoon	2.0
Pork	0
Pork liver, 4 oz. cooked	4.2
Potato chips, 10 chips	10.0
Potatoes	
baked or boiled, 1 medium with skins	21.0
canned, 4 oz. drained	11.0
French fried, fresh, 10 pieces	20.5
frozen, 10 pieces	19.2
mashed with milk and butter, ½ cup	12.8
sweet, canned, ½ cup cooked	27.1
fresh, 1 medium cooked	35.8
yams (*same as* sweet potatoes)	
Poultry	0
Preserves (*see* Jams and jellies)	
Prawns, 4 oz. cooked	1.7
Pretzels, 1 small stick	.8
Prosciutto	0
Prune juice, ½ cup	24.5
Prunes, 1 medium	4.5
½ cup cooked, unsweetened	39.0

Quail	0
Quinine water, 6 oz.	16.5
diet, 6 oz.	.8
Rabbit	0
Radishes, 1 small	.3
Raisins, ½ cup	55.7
Raspberries	
black, canned, ½ cup unsweetened	12.1
fresh, ½ cup unsweetened	10.5
red, canned, ½ cup unsweetened	10.0
fresh, ½ cup unsweetened	9.8
frozen, ½ cup sweetened	30.8
Red pepper, 1 medium	4.0
Red snapper	0
Rhubarb, ½ cup cooked sweetened	43.2
Rice	
brown, ½ cup cooked	28.9
white, ½ cup cooked	20.3
instant, ½ cup cooked	19.8
wild, ½ cup cooked	20.5
mix, ½ cup cooked	21.0
Rock Cornish game hens	0
Root beer, 6 oz.	19.5
diet, 6 oz.	.1
Rum	0
Rutabagas (*see* Turnips, yellow)	
Rye whiskey	0
Salad dressings	
fines herbes, commercial, 1 tablespoon	1.0
homemade, 1 tablespoon	.2
Green Goddess, commercial, 1 tablespoon	1.2
homemade, 1 tablespoon	.3
guacamole, 1 tablespoon	.6
French, commercial, 1 tablespoon	2.8
homemade, 1 tablespoon	.2

lime-mint, 1 tablespoon	.3
mayonnaise, homemade, 1 tablespoon	.1
real, commercial, 1 tablespoon	.2
salad dressing, commercial, 1 tablespoon	1.8
sour cream I	.5
sour cream II	.3
sweet and sour, commercial, 1 tablespoon	6.5
homemade, 1 tablespoon	.3
Roquefort, commercial, 1 tablespoon	1.0
homemade, 1 tablespoon	.2
Russian, commercial, 1 tablespoon	1.6
Thousand Island, commercial, 1 tablespoon	2.5
homemade, 1 tablespoon	.4
vinaigrette, 1 tablespoon	.3
Salads	
asparagus vinaigrette, 1 serving	5.5
avocado-watercress ring, 1 serving	8.0
beet and onion, 1 serving	8.4
broccoli, 1 serving	5.7
Caesar, 1 serving	4.1
céleri rémoulade, 1 serving	5.9
cole slaw, commercial, 1 serving	8.5
homemade, 1 serving	4.7
crab Louis, 1 serving	7.0
cucumber and onion, 1 serving	3.6
curried chicken, 1 serving	2.4
fruit, commercial, 1 serving	26.5
homemade, with julienne turkey, 1 serving	8.2
Greek, 1 serving	5.1
hearts of palm, 1 serving	3.0
macaroni, commercial, 1 serving	13.9
mushroom, sliced, 1 serving	2.5
potato, commercial, 1 serving	18.5
Salade Niçoise, 1 serving	8.5
tomato aspic, commercial, 1 serving	20.7
homemade, 1 serving	6.4

tomato stuffed with seafood, 1 serving	6.3
wilted spinach, 1 serving	3.1
Salami, 1 oz. slice	.3
Salmon, fresh and smoked	0
Sauces, dessert	
butterscotch, 1 tablespoon	20.2
fudge, 1 tablespoon	19.0
gervaise, 1 tablespoon	.4
rum custard, 1 tablespoon	.8
sabayon, 1 tablespoon	.8
strawberry chantilly, 1 tablespoon	.8
vanilla custard, 1 tablespoon	1.2
Sauces, for meats, seafood, and vegetables	
A-1, 1 tablespoon	2.7
Allemande, 1 tablespoon	.5
almond butter, 1 tablespoon	.6
barbecue, commercial, 1 tablespoon	6.2
Béarnaise, 1 tablespoon	.3
Béchamel, commercial, 1 tablespoon	1.2
homemade, 1 tablespoon	.9
beurre noir, 1 tablespoon	.3
brown sauce, commercial, 1 tablespoon	1.0
homemade, 1 tablespoon	.4
cheese, commercial, 1 tablespoon	1.0
homemade, 1 tablespoon	.7
chili, commercial, 1 tablespoon	3.8
cocktail, commercial, 1 tablespoon	3.7
cranberry, 1 tablespoon	5.3
curry, 1 tablespoon	.4
Dresden, 1 tablespoon	.5
Epicurean, 1 tablespoon	.3
garlic butter, commercial, 1 tablespoon	1.2
homemade, 1 tablespoon	.3
Heinz 57, 1 tablespoon	3.5
Hollandaise, commercial, 1 tablespoon	1.0
homemade, 1 tablespoon	.3

horseradish mousseline, 1 tablespoon	.3
lemon butter, 1 tablespoon	.2
lobster, 1 tablespoon	.5
maître d'hôtel butter, 1 tablespoon	.3
Meunière butter, 1 tablespoon	.2
Mornay, 1 tablespoon	.8
mousseline horseradish, 1 tablespoon	.3
mustard, 1 tablespoon	.5
périgueux, 1 tablespoon	.4
ravigôte, 1 tablespoon	.3
rémoulade, commercial diet, 1 tablespoon	.6
homemade, 1 tablespoon	.2
riata, 1 tablespoon	.7
seafood, 1 tablespoon	.4
shrimp, 1 tablespoon	.3
soy, 1 tablespoon	1.3
Tabasco, 1 teaspoon	.1
tartar, commercial, 1 tablespoon	.6
homemade, 1 tablespoon	.3
Velouté, 1 tablespoon	.5
verte, 1 tablespoon	.2
white, commercial, 1 tablespoon	1.2
homemade, 1 tablespoon	.9
Worcestershire, 1 tablespoon	3.6
Sauerkraut, ½ cup drained	4.7
Sausages, 1 oz.	.8
Scallions (green onions), 1 tablespoon chopped	.6
Scallops, 4 oz. cooked	3.8
Scotch whiskey	0
Scrapple, 4 oz.	16.6
Scrod	0
Seafood (see individual listings)	
Seltzer water, 8 oz.	0
Sesame seeds, 1 teaspoon	.8
Seven-Up, 6 oz.	18.0
Shad	0

Shad roe, 4 oz.	2.2
Shallots, 1 tablespoon chopped	2.4
Sherry, cocktail, 1 oz.	2.3
cream, 1 oz.	3.7
dry, 1 oz.	1.4
Shortening	0
Shrimp, canned, 4 oz.	.8
fresh, 4 oz. cooked	1.7
frozen, 4 oz. breaded	22.6
Smelts	0
Snails, canned, 4 oz.	2.3
Snow peas (*see* Peas)	
Sole	0
Soups	
avgolemono, 1 serving	3.4
Billi Bi, 1 serving	5.0
black bean, canned, 1 serving	15.3
borscht, canned, 1 serving	8.7
homemade, 1 serving	5.4
bouillon, beef, canned, 1 serving	2.8
cube or powder, 1 serving	.5
chicken, canned, 1 serving	1.9
cube or powder, 1 serving	.6
caviar Madrilène, 1 serving	3.3
chicken broth, 1 serving	.1
chicken noodle, canned, 1 serving	6.5
clam chowder, New England, canned, 1 serving	12.0
Manhattan, canned, 1 serving	9.0
consommé, beef, 1 serving	2.6
jellied, 1 serving	3.1
chicken, 1 serving	1.9
jellied, 1 serving	2.1
Madrilène, 1 serving	2.4
with quenelles, 1 serving	1.6
curried avocado, 1 serving	3.5
egg-drop, 1 serving	.3

gazpacho, 1 serving	7.8
lobster bisque, 1 serving	6.2
minestrone, canned, 1 serving	10.5
mushroom, cream, canned, 1 serving	12.0
onion, 1 serving	6.4
petite marmite, 1 serving	2.5
Philadelphia snapper, 1 serving	4.1
Senegalese, 1 serving	6.6
split pea, canned, 1 serving	15.6
tomato, cold 1 serving	7.3
creamed, canned, 1 serving	15.3
vegetable, canned, 1 serving	9.6
vichyssoise, canned, 1 serving	12.2
watercress, cream of, 1 serving	3.8
Soy sauce, 1 tablespoon	1.4
Soya powder, 1 oz.	9.6
Soybean sprouts, ½ cup cooked	.9
Spaghetti, ½ cup cooked "al dente"	21.9
½ cup cooked tender and rinsed	15.2
Spaghetti tomato or marinara sauce, ½ cup	11.4
Spareribs (pork)	0
Spices	0
Spinach	
fresh, ½ cup cooked and drained	2.8
1 cup raw and trimmed	1.4
frozen, chopped, ½ cup cooked and drained	4.2
leaf, ½ cup cooked and drained	4.4
Squab	0
Squash	
summer, ½ cup cooked	2.7
zucchini, ½ cup cooked or raw	1.9
winter, acorn, ½ cup baked	16.2
butternut, ½ cup boiled	11.8
hubbard, ½ cup boiled	8.1
Squid	0
Strawberries, fresh, ½ cup	6.0
frozen, ½ cup whole sweetened	26.6

String beans (*see* Beans, green)	
Succotash, canned, ½ cup cooked	17.6
frozen, ½ cup cooked	19.6
Sugar	
brown, 1 tablespoon	12.8
confectioners', 1 tablespoon sifted	5.9
granulated, 1 tablespoon	12.1
Sweet potatoes (*see* Potatoes)	
Sweetbreads, all kinds	0
Swiss chard, ½ cup cooked	.8
Swordfish	0
Syrups	
chocolate fudge, 1 tablespoon	7.6
corn, 1 tablespoon	15.0
grenadine, 1 tablespoon	7.6
honey, 1 tablespoon	17.2
maple, 1 tablespoon	13.0
molasses, light, 1 tablespoon	13.0
pancake, 1 tablespoon	13.5
Tabasco sauce, 1 teaspoon	.1
Tangelos, ½ cup sections	9.1
Tangerines, ½ cup sections	11.2
Tapioca, instant, 1 tablespoon	2.3
Tea, 1 cup	.1
Toast (*see* Breads—carbohydrate count not changed)	
Tomato catsup, 1 tablespoon	4.3
Tomato juice, ½ cup	5.2
Tomato paste, 1 tablespoon	2.6
Tomato purée, 1 tablespoon	1.2
Tomato sauce, 1 tablespoon	.8
Tomatoes, canned, ½ cup	5.1
½ cup stewed	7.5
½ cup Italian	4.9
cherry, 1 small	.5
fresh, 1 medium peeled	6.0
1 medium unpeeled	7.0

Tongue, beef, canned, 4 oz. cooked	.8
fresh, 4 oz. cooked	.5
Tonic water, 6 oz.	16.5
diet, 6 oz.	.8
Tripe	0
Trout	0
Truffles, canned, 1 oz.	.8
Tuna fish	0
Turkey	0
Turnip greens, ½ cup cooked	2.4
Turnips, white, ½ cup cooked	3.8
½ cup peeled raw	4.3
yellow (rutabagas)	
½ cup cooked	7.1
½ cup peeled raw strips	7.7
Turtle	0
Vanilla extract, 1 teaspoon	.1
Veal	0
Veal kidney, 4 oz. cooked	.9
V-8 juice, ½ cup	4.3
Venison	0
Vermouth, dry, 1 oz.	.5
sweet, 1 oz.	4.0
Vinegar, cider, distilled or wine, 1 tablespoon	.8
Vodka	0
Waffles, frozen, 1 medium	10.1
homemade, 1 medium	28.1
Walnuts, black, ½ cup chopped	8.8
English, ½ cup chopped	9.5
Water chestnuts, canned, ½ cup sliced	11.0
Watercress, 1 cup trimmed	1.9
Watermelon balls, ½ cup	5.1
Wax beans (see Beans)	
Wheat germ, 1 tablespoon	3.3

Wine
  champagne, domestic dry, 1 oz.   .7
    French dry, 1 oz.   .2
  dinner, dry red, 1 oz.   .1
    dry white, 1 oz.   .1
  Dubonnet, 1 oz.   4.0
  Madeira, 1 oz.   2.1
  Marsala, 1 oz.   2.3
  mountain red or white, 1 oz.   .4
  muscatel, 1 oz.   3.7
  port, 1 oz.   3.6
  rosé, 1 oz.   1.0
  sauterne, 1 oz.   1.0
  sherry, cocktail, 1 oz.   2.3
    cream, 1 oz.   3.7
    dry, 1 oz.   1.4
  vermouth, dry, 1 oz.   .5
    sweet, 1 oz.   4.0
Wild rice, ½ cup cooked   20.4
  mix, ½ cup cooked   21.0
Worcestershire sauce, 1 tablespoon   2.7

Yams (see Potatoes)
Yeast, 1 cake   1.9
  1 tablespoon dried   3.5
Yogurt, skimmed milk, ½ cup   6.4
  whole milk, ½ cup   6.0
Youngberries (see Blackberries)

Zucchini, ½ cup cooked or raw   1.9

Glossary

AU GRATIN—cooked food mixed or covered with cream or cheese sauce and baked or broiled until the surface is browned (cauliflower au gratin).

BAKE—to cook in the oven (cheese soufflé or baked ham). When applied to meats, the process is frequently called roasting (roast beef).

BARBECUE—to roast or broil on a rack or revolving spit over or under heat while basting with a sauce or marinade (barbecued spareribs).

BASTE—to moisten food with pan drippings, a liquid, or a marinade while cooking to prevent drying and to add flavor (chicken tarragon).

BEAT—to work a mixture smooth by rapid, regular movement using an electric mixer, rotary beater, wire whisk, spoon, or fork (eggs).

BLEND—to mix thoroughly two or more ingredients (garlic butter).

BOIL—to cook in liquid at boiling point which is reached when bubbles rise continuously and break on the surface of the liquid.

BRAISE—to brown meat or vegetables in hot fat or butter and cover to cook slowly, sometimes adding a liquid after the initial browning (braised Belgian endive).

225

BROIL—to cook directly under heat or over hot coals, as on a grill (broiled steak piquant).

CHILL—to allow to become cold, usually in the refrigerator.

CHOP—to cut into small pieces (onions).

CLARIFY—to render clear by separating solids from liquid (clarified butter).

COAT—to cover the surface of food evenly with flour, grated cheese or sugar (veal Parmigiana) or a spoon with thickened custard (rum custard sauce).

COMBINE—to mix all ingredients (sour cream dressing).

COOL—to let stand at room temperature until no longer warm to the touch (moules ravigote).

CREAM—to mix with a spoon or electric beater until soft, smooth and evenly blended (escargots).

CUBE—to cut into bite-size cubes (shish kebab).

DASH—a few grains of dry ingredient (cayenne pepper) or drops of liquid (Tabasco).

DICE—to cut into ¼-inch cubes (gazpacho).

DISSOLVE—to combine a dry substance and a liquid into solution (French dressing).

DOT—to scatter small amounts of butter, etc., over the surface of food (broiled salmon steak tarragon).

FLAMBÉ—to cover or combine food with brandy or cognac, ignite, and serve flaming (steak poivre, flambé).

FOLD—to combine a delicate ingredient (whipped cream or stiffly beaten egg whites) with a batter using an under-and-over motion with a rubber spatula until thoroughly blended (daiquiri lime parfait).

FRY—to cook in hot fat; also called sauté (sautéed mushrooms).

GARNISH—to decorate (watercress or lemon wedges).

GLAZE—to coat with sugar syrup or melted jelly during or after cooking (glazed carrots or ham).

GRATE—to rub on a grater to make small particles (cheese or lemon rind).

JULIENNE—to cut into narrow, lengthwise, matchlike strips (fruit salad with julienne turkey).

MARINATE—to soak food in a spicy, often acid, mixture to improve flavor and to tenderize meats (London broil).

MELT—to heat solids until they liquefy (butter or sugar).

MINCE—to cut or chop into very fine pieces (garlic).

MIX—to stir until ingredients are thoroughly combined.

PEEL—to strip or slip off the outer covering of some vegetables or fruits (beets or apples).

PINCH—the amount of a spice or herb that can be held between the thumb and forefinger (a pinch of salt).

PREHEAT—to heat oven or broiler to desired temperature before using.

PURÉE—to press food through a fine sieve or liquefy in an electric blender (Senegalese soup).

ROAST—to cook meat in the oven (roast beef): also called baking (baked ham).

REDUCE—to lessen quantity of liquid by boiling it away to a smaller concentrated amount (beef roulades).

SAUTÉ—to cook in a small amount of hot fat (sautéed mushrooms); also called frying (fried onions).

SEAR—to brown the surface of meat over high heat (sauerbraten).

SEASON—to add a sprinkling of salt and pepper to taste (seasoned flour).

SHRED—to cut or tear into long, narrow pieces (cole slaw).

SIFT—to put one or more dry ingredients through a fine sieve (seasoned flour).

SIMMER—to cook a liquid just below the boiling point (avgolemono soup).

SLIVER—to cut or split into long, thin strips (almond butter).

STIR—to mix with a spoon or a fork until ingredients are blended.

TOSS—to tumble ingredients lightly with a lifting motion (Caesar salad).

WEDGE—to cut fruit or hard-cooked eggs in the triangular shape of a wedge (prosciutto and melon).

WHIP—to beat rapidly with a wire whisk, rotary or electric beater to incorporate air and expand volume (strawberry Chantilly).

Index

Index